FLORIDA STATE
UNIVERSITY LIBRARIES

OCT 9 2000

TALLAHASSEE, FLORIDA

An Encyclopedia of American Synagogue Ritual

Kerry M. Olitzky

Marc Lee Raphael
Advisory Editor

GREENWOOD PRESS
Westport, Connecticut • London

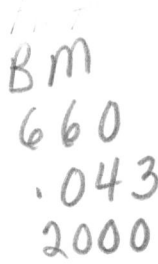

BM
660
.O43
2000

Library of Congress Cataloging-in-Publication Data

Olitzky, Kerry M.
　An encyclopedia of American synagogue ritual / Kerry M. Olitzky ; Marc Lee Raphael, advisory editor.
　　p. cm.
　Includes bibliographical references and index.
　ISBN 0–313–30814–4 (alk. paper)
　　1. Judaism—Liturgy—Encyclopedias. 2. Judaism—Liturgy—History—Encyclopedias. 3. Judaism—United States—Encyclopedias. I. Raphael, Marc Lee. II. Title.
BM660.O45　2000
296.4'5'097303—dc21　　　　99–054418

British Library Cataloguing in Publication Data is available.

Copyright © 2000 by Kerry M. Olitzky and Marc Lee Raphael

All rights reserved. No portion of this book may be reproduced, by any process or technique, without the express written consent of the publisher.

Library of Congress Catalog Card Number: 99–054418
ISBN: 0–313–30814–4

First published in 2000

Greenwood Press, 88 Post Road West, Westport, CT 06881
An imprint of Greenwood Publishing Group, Inc.
www.greenwood.com

Printed in the United States of America

The paper used in this book complies with the
Permanent Paper Standard issued by the National
Information Standards Organization (Z39.48–1984).

10 9 8 7 6 5 4 3 2 1

Contents

Acknowledgments vii

Introduction ix

The Encyclopedia 1

Index 153

Acknowledgments

This project followed me as my work took me from one community to another and then another. Thus, I must acknowledge those who participated in this project first when I was part of the faculty and administration at Hebrew Union College-Jewish Institute of Religion. In particular, I want to acknowledge the help of my former student research assistant Gary Pokras and former colleagues at the Wexner Heritage Foundation: Carolyn Levy Schrier and Lori Baron.

I also mention those colleagues who made helpful suggestions along the way as I sought out some elusive details: Rabbi Wayne Dosick, Dr. Karla Goldman, Rabbi Lawrence Hoffman, Dr. Michael A. Meyer, Kevin Profitt, and Dr. Jonathan Sarna.

My gratitude goes to Dr. Marc Lee Raphael, colleague and friend, for painstakingly editing each sentence in this volume—as he has two previous books that we prepared together. Although I take full responsibility for the conclusions, I could not have reached them without his direction and support, nor his attention to detail.

Above all I thank God for the blessings of family: Over the years, Sheryl, Avi, Jesse, and I have found the path of renewed Jewish ritual and together found spiritual renewal in the process

Rabbi Kerry M. Olitzky

Introduction

Rituals provide us with the primary foundation for religious life because they take the abstract ideas of ideologues and express them in concrete forms where humans live and interact with one another.[1] For some in this generation, rituals have developed a negative connotation. But the notion of a ritual itself is without positive or negative valuation. It may be considered value neutral until it is fleshed out within the context of a particular religious tradition. In this era of "pop psychology" laden with overanalysis of even the most basic of human behaviors, everything seems to reveal something that is mysterious and deep-seated. It is the performer of the ritual or the context in which a ritual is performed that gives it meaning and it is the ideological system that underpins the ritual that provides it with a foundation from which that meaning can emerge. Some rituals evoke this meaning immediately. Others do not. Often rituals communicate differently throughout history, even changing from positive to negative, particularly over time, as a result of a personal or community event. For example, the breaking of a glass at the end of a Jewish wedding ceremony (to mark the commemoration of the destruction of the ancient Temple in Jerusalem) changed in meaning after the modern state of Israel emerged in 1948. No longer did people have to mourn over the exile of the Jewish people from Jerusalem. Similarly, the relationship with Jerusalem took on even greater meaning after the Six Day War in 1967 when the old city of Jerusalem was united with west Jerusalem.[2]

Rituals mark the specific place that religious ideology enters the physical world where people live and work out the reality of their lives. For the practitioner of a particular faith, rituals may be more important than the ideas they represent. Rituals are the primary tools used by the practitioner to navigate the religion for his or her followers. They become prisms for these ideas. Rituals are often the grassroots response of individuals to the scholarly ideas of a particular group of people. These ideas naturally lend themselves to concrete expression. If these ideas are in accord with the philosophy of a particular religion, then the rituals abide through the generations. When they are no longer resonate with these ideas, either the religion's philosophy has to be modified to incorporate these ideas or the rituals and the ideas they represent are rejected. This is particularly difficult when the aesthetic of the ritual is appealing while, at the same time, the ideas that are being expressed by the ritual have come to be in direct opposition to the religion or the particular religious movement.

Often a group of people is defined by a particular ritual. Borrowing from the work of Mordecai Kaplan, the founder of Reconstructionist Judaism and its seminal thinker, I suggest that, with regard to Judaism, Jewish rituals are expressions of a set of ideas that define a continually evolving religious civilization.[3] This is a dynamic process. Thus, rituals continue to evolve as do the ideas they represent. So the meaning of rituals is constantly changing, but the rituals evolve on their own, as well. As a result, not all rituals find their origin in ideas and emerge from them. Instead, ideas often emerge from the practice of ritual. They cannot always be traced to the "religious academy," so to speak. I contend that ideas are frequently drawn out from the ritual by religious thinkers in an effort to understand them—or even study them. Thus, frequently, the ritual is an expression of an idea whose only articulation is in the ritual itself—until a scholar decides to turn the action into words by explaining it. Thus, the ideology evolves at a pace that may be far more accelerated than the development of the ritual. The ritual may become inadequate as a result and require further development or may be discarded in the presence of a new one.

In some cases, the ritual practice comes out of what may be called folk religion, a practice taken on by one culture that may be irrelevant (or even in opposition) to a particular religious ideology. However, those in authority (in this case, the rabbis) see that the people will be unwilling to let loose of the ritual. Thus, they elevate the ritual and give it sacred status. This happened frequently when superstitious practices surfaced in Judaism, particularly in the medieval period. The rabbis simply assigned meaning to specific rituals when the rituals preceded the ideas. Many of the individual rituals attendant to the wedding ceremony reflect this historical pattern.

RITUALS AS A PRISM FOR SELF-REFLECTION

Using rituals as prisms for introspection and self-reflection is a helpful technique for a faith community that strives to understand itself. This approach can be seen in the move toward the establishment of guiding principles among the non-Orthodox segments of the Jewish religious community over the past few years. This pattern was established by the Reform movement[4] as early as 1869 and followed by the Conservative movement[5] as recently as 1985 when it issued its statement of principles called *Emet Ve-emunah*. However, Reformers claim that the process of reforming core rituals is indigenous to Judaism and is a process started during the rabbinic period itself. It also explains why each generation attempts to add to the ritual base of any religion to give it relevancy and additional meaning. People want to see themselves and their own experience with the world reflected in ritual. This perspective is manifest in the debate among authorities over whether the Holocaust should be commemorated at Tisha B'av (marking the destruction of both Temples and other major Jewish catastrophes in history) or whether it required its own day of observance. In the establishment of Yom Hashoah (Holocaust Memorial Day), rituals had to be established. Among Reconstructionist Jews, many of these core rituals have been maintained, but they have been invested with new meaning—except in those cases where segments of the ritual come into conflict with basic movement values.

Often, people try to absorb specific rituals into their lives and integrate them into their own identity. This is not always possible, particularly as people are socialized into a certain relationship with individual rituals. For example, for a long period of time, the Reform movement was identified by its decision not to encourage the wearing of *kippot* (skullcaps) during worship. People were actually asked to remove their hats during worship in some Reform synagogues. It was also not the common practice for Reform Jews to don *tefillin* (phylacteries) as part of their morning worship routine. While this approach has changed somewhat in recent years as Reform Jews have become more comfortable as North Americans and are feverishly embracing Jewish ritual, previously these ritual objects were identified with traditional Judaism and therefore rejected by Reform Jewish ideologues. The nonparticipation in these rituals was part of the socialization process of the Reform movement, a process that has undergone radical change in the last few years. Contemporary thinkers are now looking for ways to integrate the use of these objects in the new Reform ideology as Reform Jews are now using these objects, regardless of their forbears' rejections.

Rituals can be either outwardly rejected or their relationship to a specific religion can lapse out of disuse. It is interesting to note that while there was a strong attempt by the Reform movement in Germany in the late nineteenth century to reject *brit milah* (ritual circumcision), its closeness to the folk prevented its rejection even as the philosophers of the movement argued vehemently against it as a barbaric rite.[6] More generally, Mordecai Kaplan argued that most Jewish rituals should be maintained and invested with new and therefore more relevant meaning. For example, one should maintain the kosher dietary laws (and the rituals associated with them) because their observance reminds the individual of his or her Jewish identity 24 hours a day.

Historically, we can look at rituals as a means of understanding how a group or subgroup has evolved and how the self sees itself in relationship to the group. We might also be able to project the future of a religious group based on its approach to these same rituals. For example, as more Conservative congregations adopt an egalitarian approach to worship, it seems likely that women in these congregations will take on rituals that they previously were not obligated to take on. In addition, more will begin to experiment with the use of certain ritual objects, including *tallit* (prayer shawl) and *kippah* (skullcap). Colors, patterns, and designs that are more appealing to women are already in evidence in some Conservative congregations.

THE NEXUS OF PUBLIC AND PRIVATE

While one's personal practice of ritual represents one's personal struggle with faith away from community scrutiny, synagogue rituals force this struggle to be moved from the private sphere into the public arena. However, because rituals are constantly in motion, they move back and forth between the home and synagogue. Sometimes, the move includes an adaptation of sorts, what some people may refer to as "adaptive behavior." For example, Friday evening Shabbat *kiddush* (blessing said over wine) belongs in the home. It is said at the dinner table, which has been transformed (following the destruction of the Temple) in this context into an altar of sorts, replacing the ancient sacrificial altar restricted to the Temple cult. As synagogues often provided lodging for travelers (particularly when itinerant Jews—usually peddlers—were not welcome in community lodging facilities), people began to say *kiddush* in the synagogue with their guests. They continued to say it whether or not they had already recited it in their homes. Unlike most other prayers, this reiteration of the prayer was not considered to be redundant (or worse, a "prayer said in vain," a legal definition of prayers that are unnecessarily said twice). Among Reform Jews, it was clear that this public synagogue ritual replaced the home ritual for many families and served as the model—or even precedent—for candle lighting on the Sabbath (initiated by the Reform movement in the synagogue), both of which (*kiddush* and candle lighting) continue in most Reform synagogues. However, people no longer lodge in synagogues. And *kiddush*, which is said to help usher in the Shabbat and consecrate it, is often relegated to late in the evening (sometimes at the conclusion of late night services). Nevertheless, the practice remains.

Another example of the fluidity in ritual can be seen in the *havdalah* ritual that ushers out the Sabbath while guiding the individual back into the workaday world. Reform Judaism initially rejected the rituals associated with *havdalah* in the movement's incipient stage because its ideologues could only see the background of *havdalah* mired in superstitions. In addition, *havdalah* no longer spoke to a community for which the traditional observance of the Sabbath became irrelevant. It is also true that like many rituals that grew out of folk religion, *havdalah* (the ceremony marking the end of the Sabbath and festivals and the start of rest of the week) is indeed steeped in superstition. However, in an effort to satisfy the desire of the people to retain the ritual, the rabbis—as they had done before—moved the superstitious into the world of the sacred and retained a core Jewish ritual. *Havdalah* reentered Reform practice through its youth movement whose leaders added the ritual to their program of activity, often performing it outdoors under the stars, particularly at retreats and in camp environments. Perhaps like the early rabbis, they liked its aesthetic dimension. For them, *havdalah* became more an experience of group-building than one of religious observance. Reform Jewish adults then took their lead from their younger counterparts and started to practice the ritual. The Reform thinkers then simply embraced the ritual without fully evaluating it, a posture that is gaining momentum in the movement as a way of handling other ritual practices.

Rituals frequently tend not to be jointly undertaken by groups of people. They are individual acts. However, the script that they follow allows individual participants to share in the experience in such a way as to undertake the work as a group to which the ritual calls us. This is particularly evident in the sacrificial rituals described in detail in the Torah, particularly in the book of Leviticus. And these rituals have been replaced by prayer. In prayer, the individual moves between the public and the private even in the context of community. And certain prayers, according to Jewish tradition, require a prayer quorum (*minyan*), the smallest unit of community accepted by Jewish law. The requirement of a *minyan* emerges from Abraham's argument with God over the fate of Sodom and Gomorrah and the scouts whom Moses sent out to Canaan as an advance party before entering the land. While Reform thinkers rejected the requirement of *minyan* for specific prayers, many individual synagogues still abide by this requirement and are thereby overriding the early decision by their practice even if the rabbinic governing body (which has no binding authority) has not rescinded its earlier decision. In Reform Judaism, the individual still holds sway over the group, and while the Reform movement still attends to individual choice as a *sine qua nom*, most adults simply accept the right to individual choice as a given, regardless of movement affiliation. The Conservative movement has maintained the requirement of *minyan*. However, only egalitarian congregations count women in their *minyan*.

WHAT IS RITUAL?

A religious ritual is an orchestrated routine that follows a particular pattern and is repeated according to a specific, predetermined schedule designed to actualize a religious myth or ideological platform. There may be some flexibility and personal interpretation allowed for it, specifically in the area of the embellishment of the ritual object (called *chiddur mitzvah*). A religious ritual is a sign rather than a symbol that incorporates cognitive, affective, and psychomotor elements. A symbol, on the other hand, may be considered an item that evokes an immediate visceral response for it is a sign of something that has greater meaning. If it is a sign for an entire group, then it must evoke such a response for the entire group, rather than just a select number of individuals within it. Because of the intimate relationship that people have with symbols, they tend to hold on to them tightly. And rituals themselves are filled with symbols. Thus, rituals become multilayered with meaning.

The three elements important to a ritual may not always be obvious to the participant or the observer, particularly when the rituals function well. Rituals usually emerge out of the necessities of utility. For example, in the early days in the development of the synagogue, the Torah was not kept in an ark that was housed in the synagogue. Instead, it was brought into the sanctuary space when it was needed. Often, a rolling ark of sorts was used. A small assembly gathered at the reading table and simply read from the Torah. However, as congregations grew in size and arks became permanent installations in sanctuaries, congregants felt the need to carry the Torah in a more celebratory fashion from the ark to the reading table, especially if the act of reading the Torah in public were to simulate revelation—as it was intended. Thus, the Torah circuit, or *hakafah*, was born. This ritual has a set of rules that reflect the psychomotor skills required. The Torah is taken through the congregation according to a prescribed route. People approach it to touch it or kiss it. Those who can't reach it may bow slightly as it passes without turning their backs to it. The appearance of the Torah in public pageantry communicates emotionally to people. And there are intellectual ideas about revelation that fuel the entire ritual. In an effective expression of a ritual of this sort, these elements are handled flawlessly and are well communicated. When the ritual is not performed well, the elements are not communicated and it loses its power as a ritual. It may even be said that it ceases to be a ritual according to the guidelines that have been established.

Often the Hebrew word for a particular ritual provides us with additional insight on the utility and meaning of the ritual. Ironically, there are those who argue that there is no Hebrew equivalent for the word "ritual." This is a way of expressing doubt, therefore, as to whether the notion of ritual exists as a value construct in Judaism at all. Some will suggest that rituals are limited to the dialogue between God and the individual, in contradistinction to those acts between the individual and other humans and the acts that affect only the individual and no one else. As a result, there must be no rational explanation or understanding of rituals. If there is such an understanding, then the practice under discussion cannot be a ritual. Instead, rituals emerge from Divine commandments for which all explanation is beyond the rational and therefore irrelevant.

HOW IS RITUAL DIFFERENT FROM CUSTOM, TRADITION, AND CEREMONY?

Rituals differ from customs, traditions, and ceremonies. However, often customs (and traditions) and ceremonies color rituals and distinguish one community from another. A custom may have no ideological base. It may simply be the way something has been done in a particular community and passed down through generations, thus becoming a tradition of a particular community. It starts more as a personal preference that resonates with the culture of a particular community. Or it may be the unique way one community performs a particular ritual. For example, in some homes, each Sabbath and holiday, as family members say a blessing over *challah* bread, each member of the family takes hold of the bread. If the group is large, then people grab the shoulder of the one who is closest to the bread. Once the blessing has been completed, each family member simultaneously tears a piece of bread. In other homes, the bread is simply torn by the head of the household. (Knives are not used because the Sabbath and holiday table has been transformed into an altar of sorts where weapons of war, such as knives, are prohibited.) In still other homes, the head of the house tears off a piece of bread and tosses it to those who sit around the table. (Some bakeries even prepare their *challah* with this tearing in mind.) How did any of these individual customs arise? Were they responses to specific contexts (such as large gatherings) and then became part of the family's customs? Perhaps the behaviors are linked to specific individuals in the family and maintaining the specific approach to the ritual keeps people close in memory to the one who first performed it? Without specific research on individual rituals in communities, one cannot be sure. Often one generation's creativity is the next generation's tradition.

HOW DOES RITUAL FUNCTION?

Rituals serve a simple function. They attempt to take abstract ideas and put them in a concrete form. This is particularly helpful as an educational delivery mechanism for the visual learner. In addition, it is clear that we learn much better from actually experiencing something than we do from a frontal lecture about a similar set of ideas. Rituals become part of a living classroom for religion. In religious terms, the ancient Israelites who witnessed revelation did not need the same reassurances about faith in the Almighty as did subsequent generations. Instead, they needed to rely on religious myths such as historical memory in order to affirm their faith. Rituals often remind us of incidents in the Torah and throughout Jewish history. This is particularly helpful in the affirmation of religious myths and the story of miracles. Thus, the rituals provide believers with a means to affirm their faith.

Nevertheless, just because these ideas enter the material world does not necessarily make them either accessible or easily understood, particularly when the ideas they represent are rather complex. Perhaps the goal of the ritual is to take complex religious ideas and make them easily accessible in simple human activities. The rituals simplify the idea. So when the Torah text teaches the believer that the words of the Torah should be "frontlets between your eyes," he places the *tefillin* for the head there. However, just as we have learned that rendering ideas from Hebrew into English does not make them automatically understood by the native speaker of English, moving complex ideas into rituals (which are often similarly complex) does not necessarily make them accessible either. As a matter of fact, many rituals are so elaborate that they require an educational framework in order for them to be learned. Historically, rituals were learned by watching others doing them (generally parents and relatives) and then doing them oneself. Specific education to teach a ritual (in the form of "how to" workshops) is a relatively new phenomenon in Jewish life with the possible exception of the rules of *taharat hamishpacha* (family purity).[7] It is ironic that as families participate less in the context of community, the responsibility for educating the child has been given over to that community.[8] This is particularly the case among non-Orthodox Jews.

Rituals can stand alone or be part of an array of other rituals, one dependent on the other. In the traditional world, some rituals are restricted to men or women. In the liberal context, most rituals are available equally to men and women. Yet, there is still a tendency, even among liberals, to retain the traditional stronghold on certain rituals. For example, there is nothing that prevents men from lighting Sabbath or holiday candles. Traditional men are required to do so when women are not present. Yet, it is rare that men are encouraged to light Sabbath or holiday candles, even in a liberal context, when women are present. The same thing holds true in reverse for women with regard to *kiddush* on the Sabbath or holidays. However, the restriction to men is not as limiting, and in liberal contexts, women may be more inclined to do so even in the presence of men.

THE DYNAMISM OF RITUALS

The ancient Greek philosopher Heraclitus once wrote, "You can't step in the same river twice." The same thing may be said of rituals. They are dynamic; they are not static. Each time a person performs the same ritual, it changes. Sometimes the changes are unimportant or imperceptible, but rituals change nonetheless. It is nearly impossible to do the same ritual exactly the same way each time. Rituals are not performances. They are supposed to emerge from the heart and the soul. Over time, the nuances may build to become major changes. Similarly, the relationship of the individual to the ritual changes, and the ritual takes on a lesser or greater meaning. When people are young, they may relate to a particular ritual in far different ways than when they get older.

Rituals are also responsive. Even among those who argue that these religious practices should not be changed, rituals are indeed responsive to changing times. This is part of the dynamism of religion and even a key to the survival of a particular religion. In addition, as needs arise, rituals emerge to address those needs. While this volume does not include rituals of recent origin (as they remain in wild flux and are not yet fixed), it is important to make note of them. For example, over the last twenty years, a variety of rituals has emerged to address needs expressed by the Jewish women's movement. Early on, this movement embraced Rosh Chodesh (New Moon, beginning of a new month) and claimed it as its own. In addition, as a way of expressing a variety of experiences in the context of sacred community, it looked to ritualize experiences specific to women, such as miscarriage or rape. This raised the painful experience to a sacred plain, and, in doing so, it helped to bring healing to the soul. The nascent men's movement[9], on the other hand, has not yet responded with such a plethora of rituals. Perhaps it is simply a function of time. Or perhaps these men consider Judaism itself to be male-centered and therefore see no need to add more rituals to it. Or perhaps men do not express themselves ritually in the same way as do women. Therefore, though some men are attempting to reclaim *kiddush levanah* (sanctification of the moon) as their ritual as a parallel (some may call it syncretism) to Rosh Chodesh, they have yet to find a means to ritualize those specific male experiences that may or may not parallel female experiences, such as surviving prostate cancer and dealing with penile erectile dysfunction. It is still too early to predict the outcome of male experimentation with ritual.

THE "HOW TO" OF RITUAL[10]

Each ritual can be understood in three ways: the cognitive or intellectual aspect; the affective or emotive aspect (sometimes called the spiritual); and the psychomotor (sometimes referred to as the psychospiritual). The last is the functional part of ritual, or skill set, which may even include the aesthetic, or "art form," of the ritual. People may primarily engage the ritual through one or more of its characteristics. Generally, one aspect takes precedent in the performances of the ritual. Ideally, one should engage the ritual equally through all three of its facets, but this is seldom possible. While some are satisfied with only knowing how to do a ritual, if a ritual is to be effective, it must communicate itself on all three levels without explanation. Jewish tradition argues that the repetitive doing of the ritual will lead to its eventual understanding.

The how-to aspect of a ritual is important because it more fully engages the individual than merely an intellectual exposition on the ritual. It brings the body fully into the experience in a way that ideas alone cannot do. In the beginning of the history of the Reform movement (marked by a radical approach to Jewish religion and ritual), many rituals were discarded even if some of the ideas they represented were maintained. After a short period of time, many of the ideas also fell by the way. They could not be retained by the folk as ideas when they did not take concrete form. In more recent years, many of these rituals have re-emerged in the Reform movement. In those cases where the ideas were not in accord, they were given new meaning or explained in the sphere of the metarational where rational judgments could be suspended. Among Reconstructionist Jews, rituals were maintained and given new meaning when the old meaning no longer spoke to them. In North America today, this seems to be the primary direction people are taking with regard to ritual.

THE SPIRITUAL ELEMENTS OF RITUAL[11]

For many people, ritual is part of the discipline of Jewish life. It may even help to create a rhythm for that discipline. For some, this is its spiritual element. But for others, ritual must contain a transcendent spiritual element for it to be engaging or effective. The spiritual element may be described as any mechanism that brings people closer to God. Without this element, the ritual may be considered irrelevant or ineffective. Some people use these criteria to determine whether or not they will continue to perform the ritual. If it does not move them to an elevated spiritual place, they will discontinue doing it. Rabbi Wayne Dosick suggests that rituals "are performed to bring people to a deeper place in the human psyche than words can touch. Rituals are without words, before words."[12] They reflect a part of the human being that cannot be expressed by words.

HOW DOES RITUAL DEFINE AND DEMARCATE COMMUNITY?[13]

Rituals may serve the function of marking one Jewish community from another.[14] If you do it one way, then you belong to one community. If you do it another way, this identifies you as a member of another community. Jakob J. Petuchowski argued that the Reform movement, basically constituted by immigrants from a high socioeconomic group in German society, consciously tried to keep the Eastern European lower class out of its synagogues by removing hats during worship. This proved to others that they were fully American. They prayed just like their Protestant American brethren. Thus, in its early period, the removal of hats marked the Reform movement as distinctive from the other movements. In this case, the cessation of a ritual helped to identify individuals, just as the wearing of head covering had previously separated the Jewish community from other faith communities. The *kippah* was particularly important when other identifying garments, such as the *tallit katan* (small prayer shawl generally worn under one's clothing), became undergarments rather than outer garments. In addition, the *kippah* took on additional meaning as a factor of Jewish self-identification following the Six Day War in 1967. This ritual object was appropriate and turned into a symbol of identification with the modern state of Israel.

THE BLURRING OF LINES OF COMMUNITY AND RITUAL

Many of the common assumptions that are made about synagogue ritual in North America are filtered through the lens of the Ashkenazic community, those Jews whose community roots can be traced back to Central and Eastern Europe. However, there are other communities, most notably the Sephardic (those who are descended from Spain) and what are known as *Edot haMizrach* (or eastern communities that include Arab lands) who express themselves ritually in ways markedly different from those of Ashkenazic communities and have a slate of rituals that have not found their way into Ashkenazic congregations at all. Some of these have been influenced by their lands of origin and the interaction with other peoples. Others have developed on their own, following paths different from the rest of the world Jewish community.

THE RECLAMATION OF RITUAL

The Jewish community is full of buzz words: concepts that reflect the latest trends in organized Jewish life.[15] Some of these are championed by the organized Jewish community represented primarily by local Jewish Federations. They may even be financial campaign slogans. Others are simply North American ideas that are given Jewish filters, such as might be said of the baby boomer interest in spirituality. For a period of some years recently, "Jewish continuity" was the buzz word. Today it is "renaissance," which is typified by the embrace of traditional Jewish ritual in a wide variety of contexts that transcends communities and congregations that are known to be part of the Jewish renewal movement as it calls itself.

Clearly, there is a generational element at play in this renaissance. Feeling secure as North Americans, the current generation is prepared to embrace Jewish rituals that formerly separated members of the Jewish community from the mainstream and were therefore rejected. Now young Jews are embracing those rituals that affirm their Jewish identities and, as a result, potentially distance them from the mainstream that their parents worked hard to claim as their own.

ABOUT THIS VOLUME

This volume includes those practices that emerge out of synagogue life. However, as there is historical fluidity between what takes place in the home and the synagogue, some of the rituals may find their place in the Jewish home in this generation while in the synagogue in another. Others are expressed in both places. While it is our intention to comment on the different practices among the various religious movements or streams in the Jewish community, often practices vary from congregation to congregation rather than from movement to movement. In these cases, no comment is made.

Entries in this volume are listed in alphabetical order. Whether the English or Hebrew (or Yiddish) term is given as the primary reference is determined by common usage. For cross-referencing purposes, bold face type is used to indicate a main entry for the term.

NOTES

1. See these seminal works on ritual: Mary Douglas, *Natural Symbols, Explorations in Cosmology* (New York: Routledge, 1996); Tom Driver, *The Magic of Ritual* (San Francisco: Harper San Francisco, 1991); Mircea Eliade, *The Sacred and the Profane* (New York: Harcourt, Brace and World, 1959); Clifford Geertz, *Interpretation of Culture* (New York: Basic Books, 1977). For an application of these works to the place of rituals in Jewish life, see the various works of Lawrence A. Hoffman. In particular, see Lawrence A. Hoffman, *The Art of Public Prayer: Not for Clergy Only*, 2nd edition (Woodstock, VT: Jewish Lights Publishing, 1999); Lawrence A. Hoffman, *Beyond the Text: A Holistic Approach to Liturgy* (Bloomington, IN: Indiana University Press, 1990).

2. For a legal treatment, see Norman Lamm, *The Jewish Way in Love and Marriage* (New York: Harper and Row, 1992). For a more popular treatment on the ritual of marriage, see Norman Lamm, *A Hedge of Roses, Jewish Insights into Love and Marriage* (New York: Feldheim Publishers, 1997). For a comparative look at marriage and other life cycle events, see Paul F. Bradshaw and Lawrence A. Hoffman, eds., *Life Cycle in Jewish and Christian Worship* (South Bend, IN: University of Notre Dame Press, 1998).

3. On Kaplan and Reconstructionism, see Jeffrey Gurock and Jacob J.

Schacter, *A Modern Heretic and a Traditional Community: Mordecai Kaplan, Orthodoxy and American Judaism* (New York: Columbia University Press, 1998). For an intellectual biography of Kaplan, see Mel Scult, *Judaism Faces the 20th Century: A Biography of Mordecai M. Kaplan* (Detroit: Wayne State University Press).

4. On the Reform movement's approach to ritual as a reflection of its ideology in a popular form, see Eugene B. Borowitz, *Liberal Judaism* (New York: UAHC Press, 1990). For an extensive treatment of the history of ideas in the Reform movement, see Michael A. Meyer, *Response to Modernity: A History of the Reform Movement in Judaism* (Detroit: Wayne State University Press, 1994).

5. On the Conservative movement's practical treatment of ritual, see Isaac Klein, *A Guide to Jewish Religious Practice* (Hoboken, NJ: KTAV Publishing Co., 1988).

6. For an analysis of the Reform movement's attitude toward *brit milah*, see Lewis Barth, ed., *Berit Milah in a Reform Jewish Context* (NP, Berit Milah Board of Reform Judaism, 1990). For a general approach to the subject, see Lawrence A. Hoffman, *Covenant of Blood: Circumcision and Gender in Rabbinic Judaism* (Chicago: University of Chicago Press, 1995).

7. For a fuller understanding of the laws of ritual purity, see Hyam MacCoby, *Ritual and Morality and Its Place in Judaism* (Cambridge: Cambridge University Press, 1999).

8. For a treatment of this subject of introducing children to Jewish education in the medieval period, see Ivan G. Marcus, *Rituals of Childhood: Jewish Culture and Acculturation in Medieval Europe* (New Haven: Yale University Press, 1998).

9. For a discussion of some of the basic questions facing this incipient Jewish men's movement, see Kerry M. Olitzky, *From Your Father's House, Reflections for Jewish Men* (Philadelphia: Jewish Publication Society, 1999). The introduction includes a brief history of the movement.

10. For a demonstration of this basic approach to Jewish ritual, see Kerry M. Olitzky and Ronald Isaacs, *The How To Handbook of Jewish Living*, Vols. I, II (Hoboken, NJ: KTAV Publishing Co., 1993, 1996).

11. See the works of Lawrence A. Kushner, as well as the back list of Jewish Lights Publishing for many examples of spirituality and ritual and Jewish religion. Also, see Arnold Rosenberg, *Jewish Liturgy as a Spiritual System* (Northvale, NJ: Jason Aronson, 1996).

12. Wayne Dosick, *Living Judaism* (San Francisco: HarperSan Francisco, 1995), 36. Dosick's volume is representative of the spirituality that has swept the Jewish community in North America.

13. For an excellent introduction to the subject, see Arnold Eisen, *Taking Hold of Torah: Jewish Commitment and Community Today* (Bloomington, IN: Indiana University Press, 1997).

14. See Daniel Frank, ed. *A People Apart: Choseness and Ritual in Jewish Philosophical Thought* (Albany: State University of New York Press, 1993).

15. See Riv Ellen Prell, *Fighting to Become Americans: Jews, Gender and the Anxiety of Assimilation* (Boston: Beacon Press, 1999).

A

ALIYAH. A Torah honor, literally "going up" to the Torah. The term refers to the act of ascending the *bimah* (the raised platform on which the Torah is read, either in the front of the synagogue or in its center) in order to say the appropriate blessings before and after a section of the weekly Torah reading is read aloud. Originally, while individuals read the prayers from a standing desk, they ascended an elevated platform to read the Torah. An officiant called them to read from the Torah scroll when more people in the community were able to do so. The word *aliyah* is also used to describe the process of immigration to Israel, probably a result of the climbing necessary in the Judean Hills to reach the ancient Temple in Jerusalem during the thrice-yearly pilgrimages on the festivals of Sukkot, Pesach, and Shavuot. Torah *aliyot* (plural of *aliyah*) are distributed according to a specific formula but only when the Torah is to be read publicly with a *minyan*.

The Reform movement rejected the requirement of *minyan*. However, recently some Reform congregations reintroduced the idea and count women as part of the requirement. Reconstructionist congregations include women in the *minyan* as do many Conservative congregations. Orthodox synagogues do not. And women in these nonegalitarian congregations may not read from the Torah nor be called for an *aliyah*. Because the Torah reading takes place in public, the entire Jewish community should be represented. Thus, those given the honor of an *aliyah* are called up in a specified order by the *gabbai* (the caretaker/supervisor of the Torah service) using a traditional formula. In some Reform congregations, the traditional formula is not used. An individual is called by his Hebrew name, as son (and now daughter, in the egalitarian circles) of his father. There is a debate as to whether individuals in egalitarian congregations should be called to an *aliyah* in the name of both parents (as is usually the case) because mothers' names are traditionally reserved for individuals called only when prayers of healing are to be offered. In some congregations, individuals are called up in reference to their *aliyah* rather than their Hebrew names, often to protect them from possible embarrassment should a person not know his or her Hebrew name or the Hebrew name of the parent. As a matter of convenience, it is a practice among some congregations (certainly not the majority) to name all of the individuals to come up at the beginning of the reading of the Torah in order to save time in the process.

Originally, no systematic order informed the calling out of Torah honors. Usually, the one calling out the honors, the *gabbai*, called an esteemed member of the community first to read. Later, the *gabbai* called up to read first a descendant of the priestly class (the *kohanim*), followed by an individual whose ancestry could be traced to the Levites (the assistants to the priests in the ancient Temple). Finally, the *gabbai* called a commoner or ordinary Israelite. If a Kohen (singular form of *kohanim*) was not available, then the Levite *aliyah* took precedence. If a Levite was not available, a Kohen could be called up for the second *aliyah* as well as the first, but a Kohen could not be called up for an Israelite *aliyah*. This formula still prevails in Orthodox and Conservative congregations. However, because the Reform and Reconstructionist movements rejected the notion of any social class distinctions, they do not recognize individual lineage when calling people to the Torah and thus do not distinguish among *aliyot*.

According to the traditional formula, when the Torah is read on Mondays and Thursdays (designated as market days and fulfilling the Talmudic requirement [Babylonian Talmud, Bava Kamma 82a] that the Torah should be read at least once every three days), at least three people are called to the Torah. However, more people than the required minimum can be given *aliyot*. In those cases, the *gabbai* pauses briefly between the seventh and any additional *aliyot*. On the Sabbath, seven people are called to the Torah. The person who will be reading the **haftarah** (weekly lesson from the Prophets read on Shabbat and holidays) is called as the eighth person, designated as the *maftir* (the one who reads the additional reading). According to tradition, the third and sixth *aliyot* are reserved for those of great learning and piety. On Shabbat afternoon when the Torah is also read, only three *aliyot* are called. On new moons and the intermediate days of Sukkot and Pesach, there are four *aliyot*. On holidays there are five *aliyot*. And on Yom Kippur, there are six *aliyot*.

When ascending the *bimah* for an *aliyah*, one is required to take the shortest route to the Torah. If the community does not have an established pattern (called a *minhag hamakom*, literally "custom of the place"), then the individual ascends to the Torah reader's right and descends to the reader's left. While saying the blessing before the Torah reading, the individual takes a **tzitzit** (corner fringe) from the **tallit** (prayer shawl) he is wearing (or the Torah binder as is the practice for women in some egalitarian congregations when the *tallit* is not worn) and touches the place where the reading is to begin. (Often the person honored with an *aliyah* in a Reform congregation is neither wearing a *tallit* nor prepared to kiss the garment used to touch the Torah.) Most Reconstructionist congregations amended the traditional blessing before the Torah reading by excising the line that names the Jewish people as God's chosen people. Next the individual takes hold of the Torah handles (*atzei chayim*), and sometimes slightly lifts them, then stands to the right of the reader, where he or she remains during the reading. This is done because the person honored with the *aliyah* at one time actually read from the Torah. Now the Torah reader acts on his or her behalf. At the end of the reading of that section, the person honored with the *aliyah* again touches the place in the Torah where the reader concluded (kisses the garment used to touch the Torah), takes hold of the *atzei chayim* once again, and recites the concluding blessing. Then that individual moves to the left of the Torah reader and remains there until the following *aliyah* is concluded. At that time, the individual descends the *bimah*. In many communities, the individual descends the *bimah* backwards, because one is not supposed to turn one's back on the Torah.

As part of the Torah service, those given *aliyah* honors act as legal witnesses to the Sinai experience, which is being re-enacted as the public reading of the Torah. As a result, the laws concerning witnesses are also in force when distributing *aliyah* honors. While most congregations relaxed these requirements because it may be remnant of a superstition concerning the evil eye, the requirement would mean, for example, that a son may not follow his father with an *aliyah* honor. When inviting people for the honor of an *aliyah*, the traditional priority list is as follows: bridegroom (who comes to the Torah on the Sabbath prior to the wedding); bar mitzvah; baby naming (traditionally a father following the birth of a daughter); a person commemorating a **yahrzeit** (anniversary of a death); and a person rising from **shiva** (the first week of mourning). Of course, in Reform, Reconstructionist, and some Conservative congregations where men and women are treated equally, these honors would include women as well as men. It is a growing practice in some congregations to invite people for an *aliyah* as a group rather than individually. Some still call an individual even if other family members accompany the individual to the *bimah*.

Following the *aliyah*, there is a culture of praising those who have been honored with the *aliyah*. This takes several forms in addition to the blessing that may be offered on behalf of the one who has had the *aliyah* or on behalf of someone chosen by the honoree. Since the Middle Ages, honorees made a contribution to the synagogue in response, something that turned into an auction of sorts in later years and was discontinued by the Reform movement. Congregants extend their hands and say, "*Yishar koach* (May God strengthen you)," to which the individual responds, "*Barukh tihyeh* (May it be blessedly so)."

REFERENCES

Elbogen, Ismar. *Jewish Liturgy: A Comprehensive History*. Philadelphia and New York: The Jewish Publication Society and The Jewish Theological Seminary of America, 1993.

AUFRUF. The term comes from the Yiddish *oyfrufn*, "to be called up," derived from the German for "call" (*rufen*) and "up" (*auf*). The country of origin of the speaker would dictate how it is to be pronounced and thus transliterated into English. It refers specifically to the Torah honor bestowed upon the groom-to-be in Yiddish- and German-speaking Ashkenazi communities on the Shabbat prior to his wedding. It probably originated as a public announcement of a wedding and served a legal function. Some scholars suggest that its origins in medieval Germany and France are directly related to the responsibility of the community leader to determine that the proposed marriage was permitted by the Jewish law. Others trace the custom to a Talmudic story that relates how King Solomon built a gate at the Temple where the residents of Jerusalem and pilgrims would come and sit on the Sabbath to perform kind deeds to bridegrooms who would come there (Babylonian Talmud, Soferim 19). Following the destruction of the synagogue, the sages decreed that the grooms should come to the synagogue to be honored.

It is not necessary for a Torah honor to be given to the groom on Shabbat. Instead, some communities honor the individual on another Torah reading day, such as the Monday or Thursday prior to the wedding. It is traditional for the groom to receive the *maftir* **aliyah** (the *aliyah* designated for the person to read the haftarah, the weekly lesson from the Prophets read on Shabbat and holidays) if he is able to chant the **haftarah**. Following his recitation of the Torah blessing at the conclusion of his *aliyah*, he is blessed (usually by the rabbi).

According to *Machzor Vitry*, a classic and therefore authoritative prayer book for the holidays, the groom entered the synagogue for his *aufruf* accompanied by ushers and was given a seat next to the ark. The service included special prayers in honor of the couple to be married and a special reading from Isaiah 61. Following the Torah blessings, worshipers threw raisins and nuts, part of a Gematria (numerology)-inspired custom that suggested to the couple that they could determine whether the marriage would be good or bad; it could be either. It may also have significance as an omen of fertility. Although the original meaning may be lost, this practice is often followed in traditional congregations. In some communities, probably influenced by Sephardic tradition, candy has replaced nuts and raisins as a symbol of sweetness. In Reform, Reconstructionist, and egalitarian Conservative synagogues, both men and women are called to the honor of the Torah and are blessed as a couple in anticipation of their upcoming wedding. In some Reform congregations, the couple is blessed on Friday evenings; this blessing is unrelated to the reading of the Torah (which traditionally does not take place during the evening). In some congregations, it is not customary for more than one person to receive an individual *aliyah*. In this case, one of the couple receives the *aliyah* and then the couple is blessed after that individual concludes the blessing following the reading of the Torah. Following the worship service, a collation called a **kiddush** (sanctification of the wine) luncheon (because it generally begins with that ritual) is usually held to honor the couple about to be married.

REFERENCES

Diament, Anita. *The New Jewish Wedding*. New York: Summit Books, 1985.

Goldstein, Sidney E. *Meaning of Marriage and Foundations of the Family: A Jewish Interpretation*. New York: Bloch Publishing Co., 1942.

Goodman, Philip and Hanna. *The Jewish Marriage Anthology*. Philadelphia: The Jewish Publication Society of America, 1965.

Routtenberg, Lilly S., and Ruth R. Seldin. *The Jewish Wedding Book*. New York: Schocken Books, 1967.

B

BAR/BAT MITZVAH. Literally "son/daughter of the commandment," a rite of passage established for girls at age 12 (and one day) and boys at 13 (and one day) that marks the transition between childhood and the acceptance of the religious obligations and responsibilities of adulthood. While the change in status was presumed and even mentioned in the Babylonian Talmud (Bava Metzia 96a), we have no evidence of this notion of religious and legal maturity as formally assumed in a ceremony of any sort before the fourteenth century; any celebration concerning girls is not mentioned before the nineteenth century. However, there is some indication that the origin of the Bar Mitzvah ceremony in its simplest form can be traced back to antiquity. The age of 13 as a significant moment in the life of an adolescent male is mentioned in the Mishnah, Pirke Avot 5:21, obligating the male with *mitzvot* (commandments, plural of *mitzvah*) for the first time in his life. It is clear that the age of majority for the Bible occurred at 20, not 13 (see Numbers 14:29). Most liberal synagogues do not make a distinction between the ages of boys and girls. Traditionally, this meant that a boy achieving Bar Mitzvah could be a member of a *bet din* (religious court), reckoned as part of a *minyan*, could take vows and be permitted to buy and sell property. However, the authorities suggest that his testimony is not valid regarding real estate, because he is not knowledgeable in that area.

Whether marked by a ceremony or not, the Bar/Bat Mitzvah is an automatic period of transition. However, many synagogues make specific educational and attendance requirements before allowing the student to participate in such a ceremony. Ironically, it was traditionally the time in which the student *entered* formal religious education; parents provided education in the early years of a child's life. Other important aspects of the transition include the obligation of the adult male to don **tefillin** on a daily basis (excluding the Sabbath and holidays). However, when and how this is to be acted upon varies in certain communities. Sephardim and some Hasidim believe that the boy may not use *tefillin* even one day before his Bar Mitzvah. Thus, some Sephardim include the wearing of *tefillin* (not on the Sabbath) as part of the ceremony itself and honor a scholar with the task of helping the boy to wear them properly. Chabad Hasidim permit the use of *tefillin* two months before the Bar Mitzvah, but the boy may only say the appropriate blessing for one month in advance.

Among Moroccan Jews, the Bar Mitzvah takes place once the boy has reached the age of 12. He learns a Talmudic treatise, and after he is tested on the material by the rabbi and community leaders, he is invited to a dinner on the Wednesday before the Sabbath on which he is given an ***aliyah***. At the service the following morning, the rabbi places the *tefillin* on his head and his father places the *tefillin* on his arm. The choir accompanies this ceremony with a hymn. Then the boy is given an *aliyah* and must teach something that he has learned. This is followed by a discussion at the end of which he is blessed by the entire congregation. The boy then takes his *tefillin* bag and collects coins from those in attendance. A breakfast follows and then on the Sabbath he reads the **haftarah**. When he is called up to the Torah, a special *piyyut* (liturgical poem) is read.

The ceremony for boys as we know it probably dates back to the Middle Ages, perhaps in competition with the Church; girls joined in marking the moment with celebration in the early part of the twentieth century. Even in the period of the Second Temple, the sages blessed a boy at age 12 or 13 after completing his first fast day. Ben Ish Chai, a nineteenth-century halachist (legalist) from Baghdad, specifies the liturgy simply with the *barukh shepatarani* (Praised are You for releasing me from this obligation) blessing said by parents. He also advocates a festive meal following the liturgy. Ben Ish Chai can also be credited with being the first to suggest a minimal ritual for girls, which included dressing her in Sabbath clothes, blessing a new garment, and focusing on the new *mitzvot* whose obligation she assumes. However, the Bat Mitzvah itself was introduced by Rabbi

Mordecai M. Kaplan in the United States for his own daughter in the 1920s.

In some congregations, there is no real distinction made between the birthday as marked by either the secular or the Hebrew soli-lunar calendar. (The full participation of girls is still limited in some liberal synagogues and is often nonexistent in Orthodox congregations.) However, Orthodox and most Conservative congregations still make the distinction between girls and boys with regard to their majority age. The Reform and Reconstructionist movements recognize the equality of both boys and girls in this regard. In its early years, Reform Judaism generally discarded the Bar Mitzvah in favor of **Confirmation** (which took place in ninth and now in tenth grade as a group ceremony, regardless of the age of the student), but lay leaders led the initiative to reintroduce Bar Mitzvah over the last generation. Because of the concern for equality, some Reformers were concerned over the reintroduction of Bar Mitzvah. This was mitigated by the later introduction of the Bar Mitzvah, something that early Reformers had previously considered irrelevant. Others applauded the reintroduction of the Bar Mitzvah in Reform Judaism as a vehicle for saving (or resurrecting) the Saturday morning service, which had been eclipsed by the introduction of the late Friday service.

The ceremony is identified primarily as the first time an individual is called up for an *aliyah* to the reading of the Torah and to recite the appropriate blessings in the midst of regular communal worship. Going up to the Torah demonstrates the new role as a full member of the community. At that time, the father (and in liberal circles either or both parents) offers the *barukh shepatarani* prayer releasing him (or them) from specific parental responsibility. In most liberal communities, a prayer from the heart is offered in its stead. In addition, the Torah may be taken from the ark and handed to representatives of succeeding generations of the family before the Torah is given to the Bar/Bat Mitzvah for the Torah processional. (This has come to be known as the "Torah transmission ceremony.") Often the rabbi offers a sermon that includes a charge to the Bar Mitzvah. These words might be concluded with the priestly benediction, or the *mi sheberekh* (literally, "the One who blesses") blessing. Often the Bar/Bat Mitzvah offers his or her own words of teaching (called a *tefillin derasha* in the Sephardic communities and offered following the service during the meal) and of thanks. Sometimes, the new adult offers a prayer in front of the ark. In many communities, the congregation (and some of the auxiliary organizations, such as men's club or sisterhood) present the Bar/Bat Mitzvah with a gift. Following the conclusion of the service, the sharing of a meal to honor the fulfilling of a religious obligation (*seudat mitzvah*) has been transformed into a lavish celebration in many communities.

In Eastern Europe, the boy was usually called up on the Monday or Thursday (when Torah is read in the morning service) after his birthday. Then on the Sabbath, the boy would read the *maftir* (final section of the regular Torah reading) and the *haftarah* (assigned selection from the Prophets). In Lithuania and in Israel, the boy read the *maftir* just before he turned 13 and then he received an ordinary *aliyah* after his thirteenth birthday. During the seventeenth and eighteenth centuries, it became common for boys to conduct the entire worship service and, in some communities, to read the entire weekly Torah portion. In Morocco, it was a popular practice for a special *piyyut* to be read in honor of the celebration.

When Bat Mitzvah was introduced into the Conservative movement, it typically took place on Friday evening, as the service itself was out of the norm of traditional observance. Thus, the addition of a new institution was easier to make. However, as late Friday evening services declined in the Conservative movement, the Bat Mitzvah was formally accepted into the Saturday morning service in 1981, with the young woman reading only the haftarah.

REFERENCES

Cooper, John. *The Child in Jewish History*. Northvale, NJ: Jason Aronson, Inc., 1996.

Goldin, Barbara Diamond. *Bat Mitzvah: A Jewish Girl's Coming of Age*. New York: Viking Press, 1995.

Joselit, Jenna Weissman. *The Wonders of America: Reinventing Jewish Culture 1880–1950*. New York: Hill and Wang, 1994.

Salkin, Jeffrey. *Putting God on the Guest List: How to Reclaim the Spiritual Meaning of Your Child's Bar and Bat Mitzvah*. Woodstock, VT: Jewish Lights Publishing, 1992 (rev. 1996).

Schoenfeld, Stuart. "Folk Judaism, Elite Judaism and the Role of Bar Mitzvah in the Development of the Synagogue and Jewish School in America." *Contemporary Jewry* vol. 9, no. 1 (Fall/Winter 1987–1988): 67–85.

BEDECKEN. From the Yiddish "to cover," the custom of veiling of the bride, done by the groom prior to the wedding ceremony. It is derived from Genesis 24:65 when Rebecca "took a veil and covered herself" before meeting Isaac for the first time. The veiling became a sign of bridal modesty. The custom evolved that community leaders would accompany the groom as he greeted and welcomed the bride and then placed a veil over her face. However, it is popularly understood to be derived from Laban's deception of Jacob as he sought to marry Rachel and was forced initially to marry Leah. This allows the groom to be sure exactly who he is marrying. Lauterbach argues that this ceremony finds its roots in the ancient belief that the groom and bride are in mortal danger and have to protect (cover) themselves from the demons who seek to destroy them.

Today, the *bedecken* usually takes place just before the wedding processional, following the signing of the **ketubah** (marriage contract). In the presence of parents and immediate family, the groom veils the bride. He then blesses her with the words offered to Rebecca as she left her home, "O sister, may you grow into myriads" (Genesis 24:60), followed by the traditional blessing offered by parents to daughters, "May God make you as Sarah, Rebecca, Rachel, and Leah." The priestly benediction (Numbers 6:24–26) is added as well.

An increasing number of couples in the liberal community have reintroduced this aspect of the wedding, and it remains a common practice among Orthodox Jews.

REFERENCES

Diament, Anita. *The New Jewish Wedding*. New York: Summit Books, 1985.
Goodman, Philip and Hanna. *The Jewish Marriage Anthology*. Philadelphia: The Jewish Publication Society of America, 1965.
Klein, Isaac. *A Guide to Jewish Religious Practice*. New York: The Jewish Theological Seminary of America, 1979.
Lauterbach, Jacob. "The Ceremony of Breaking a Glass at Weddings." *Hebrew Union College Annual* vol. II (1925): 351–380.
Routtenberg, Lilly S., and Ruth R. Seldin. *The Jewish Wedding Book*. New York: Schocken Books, 1967.

BEDIKAT CHAMETZ. Finding or examining (*bedikah*) leavened products (*chametz*) the night before Passover in a ritualized search through the house. The *chametz* is generally defined as the leavened product that results when the grains of wheat, rye, barley, oats, or spelt come into contact with water for more than a minimum of eighteen minutes. Thus, food made from these grains is prohibited during Passover. In addition, Ashkenazi Jews do not eat rice, corn, peas, and peanuts (or any derivatives thereof), because flour ground from these vegetables and the breads baked from them would look like the breads of pure *chametz*, which might be confusing to people. This search is the final act after thorough "spring-cleaning" that is done in anticipation of Passover. Floors are vacuumed and shelves are scrubbed. Then according to the Mishnah (Pesachim 1:1), we are instructed to search for the *chametz* by the light of a flame. Some insure that bread crumbs will be found by placing them in conspicuous places around the house. This provides *chametz* so that a blessing will not be recited in vain. It is customary not to speak during the search except about matters related to the search.

As night falls on the thirteenth of Nisan, the family searches for *chametz*, using a candle to illumine dark corners; a feather, which acts as a broom; and a wooden spoon into which pieces of bread are scooped. A blessing is recited before the actual search. After the family collects the *chametz*, members of the family gather together in order to renounce all ownership of it (***bitul chametz***), using a traditional Aramaic formula called *kol chamira* after its first two words. The next morning the *chametz* is burned (***biur chametz***), often in a small bonfire at the home or the synagogue. If the night of Passover coincides with the Sabbath, the *chametz* is searched for on Thursday evening and burned on Friday morning. In many communities, the rabbi "buys" the remaining *chametz* that might still be in one's home and then "sells" (***mekhirat chametz***) collectively to a non-Jew. This process was also enacted to avoid financial loss from the (primarily commercial) destruction of large quantities of *chametz*. It guarantees that no *chametz* will be in the possession of the householder during the holiday. Most Reform Jews do not go to this extent to rid their homes of leavened foods in anticipation of Passover.

There is a second level of explanation for *chametz* that has gained renewed prominence in the contemporary generation of spiritual searching. It envisions the psychological dimension of *chametz* as the stuff of self we have left standing, which stagnates and putrefies, which we must also rid ourselves of before we can be fully free. The "evil impulse" (*yetzer harah*) is metaphorically called "leaven" in the sense of a fermenting passion (see Babylonian Talmud, Berakhot 17a) that prevents the individual from doing the will of God. Thus, just as the individual must remove the *chametz* by the light of the candle, we must remove the evil of the heart through the light of conscience, which is the "lamp of God" (Proverbs 20:27).

REFERENCES

Birnbaum, Philip. *A Book of Jewish Concepts*. New York: Hebrew Publishing Co., 1975.
Goodman, Philip. *The Passover Anthology*. Philadelphia: The Jewish Publication Society of America, 1961.
Greenberg, Irving, *The Jewish Way: Living the Holidays*. New York: Summit Books, 1988.
Strassfeld, Michael, *The Jewish Holidays: A Guide and Commentary*. New York: Harper & Row, 1985.
Waskow, Arthur I. *Seasons of Our Joy: A Handbook of Jewish Festivals*. New York: Summit Books, 1986.

BENCHEN GOMEL (BIRKAT HAGOMEL). From the Yiddish *benchen* (saying a blessing) and the Hebrew *gomel* (for showing favor), *Benchen* is derived from the Latin *benedicere* (to bless) by way of Old French. Among Sephardic Jews, the term used is *bençao*. In the case of recovery from great illness, rescue from grave danger, and release from an imprisonment, the blessing is to be said by men and women (including after childbirth) in front of a *minyan*. Because of the requirement of *minyan*, the blessing—*birkat hagomel*—is often recited during the Torah service after the one who is to offer the blessing has received an ***aliyah***. It is to be said after the second *aliyah* blessing. However, it may be said in any place where a minimum of ten individuals can be assembled for a prayer quorum. Using the traditional form of blessing, the individual thanks God for bestowing favor, and the congregation responds by asking God to continue to bestow kindness on the individual who is saying the blessing.

Since the Reform movement rejected the requirement of *minyan* early in its history, many congregations will invite an individual to recite *birkat hagomel* whether or not there are ten people assembled for prayer. However, some Reform congregations have reinstated the requirement of *minyan*.

REFERENCE

Bleich, J. David. "*Birkat Ha-Gomel* and *Tefillat Ha-Derekh* for Air Travelers." *Tradition* vol. 23, no. 3 (1988): 109–115.

BIRKAT HACHODESH. Literally "blessing of the month" (or moon), this ritual of "announcing the new moon" takes place on the Sabbath prior to Rosh Chodesh (new month). As a result, the Sabbath takes on the name Shabbat Mevarkhim (the Sabbath of Blessing) when this ritual is incorporated each month. Only on Shabbat Hachodesh, the Sabbath prior to the month of Tishrei (which begins with Rosh Hashanah on the first of the month), is this practice deemed unnecessary and therefore not required. Some scholars suggest that the entire *birkat hachodesh* (blessing of the new month) ritual is a remnant of the superstition that should the announcement of the new month not be made, Satan would become confused. This would be particularly important at the time of the impending High Holidays when people are to be judged. While Ashkenazi Jews still consider this as "blessing the new month," Sephardic prayer books refer to the ritual as "announcing the new month."

When the new month was fixed by observation of witnesses (of the new moon), its actual arrival was determined by the Sanhedrin (Rabbinic court and legislative body), which announced the new month with blessings and praise. This was necessary because the moon takes 29½ days to circle the earth. Thus, the new moon is visible after 29 or 30 days. This astronomical average was maintained by developing a calendar with months that alternated between 29 and 30 days. When the calendar became fixed in the fourth century C.E., as introduced by Hillel II, the custom developed (probably in the geonic period, 589–1038) to announce the new month on the preceding Sabbath in the synagogue during morning worship. The geonic period takes its name from the leader of the academy, the gaon, who thereby serves as community leader. It was probably a simple announcement at first, much like the community announcements that are included at the end of many worship services in synagogues today. However, it is clear that this practice was fixed by the rabbis as a way of formalizing the acceptance of fixed calendation of the Sanhedrin and the rejection of the continued need for witnesses advocated by the Karaites (sect which opposed Rabbinic law and authority by affirming only the written law of the Torah).

Although the calendar was fixed, there were no printed calendars, and the information had to be transmitted to the people so that they would know to add the *musaf* (additional) service and recite the Hallel psalms (a select group of psalms added to the liturgy on specific days). Traditionally, women also did not work on Rosh Chodesh. The ritual takes place immediately following the reading of the **haftarah** before the Torah is returned to the ark. Everyone stands for this ritual, because the Torah is held aloft during it. While another individual holds the Torah, the *shaliach tzeebor* (leader of prayer service), using a specific formula, announces the specific day(s) on which, during the upcoming week, Rosh Chodesh will fall. Two short prayers are said. Next the *shaliach tzeebor* takes the Torah, makes the announcement, and then recites a specific blessing, which is then repeated by the congregation. While the first prayer is ancient (taken from the Talmud, recast into first person plural with a few additional words, and attributed to Rav who said it as a personal prayer following the *Amidah*, the core prayer in the worship service), it was introduced into the *siddur* (prayer book) in the middle of the eighteenth century. The second prayer may date from the introduction of the announcement itself into the synagogue service. Among Lubavitch Hasidim and Sephardim, the second prayer is not included. However, in the Sephardic community, several other short prayers replace it, asking for the welfare of the rabbis, their disciples, and their families. An eleventh-century version of the second prayer, included in *Machzor Vitry*, stresses the permanent bond between all Jews and the city of Jerusalem. The prayer following the announcement is more extensive among Sephardim, Hasidim, and in Israeli congregations.

Some congregations add the *el malei rachamim* ("God who is full of compassion") prayer for those community members whose **yahrzeit** may fall during the upcoming month. Afterwards, the ritual for the Torah service continues to its conclusion.

REFERENCE

Elbogen, Ismar. *Jewish Liturgy: A Comprehensive History*, translated by Raymond P. Scheindlin. Philadelphia: Jewish Publication Society, 1993, pp. 103–104.

BIRKAT HAMAZON. Grace after meals, literally "the blessing for a portion" (of food), which emphasizes the sacred character of the meal, is considered to be the core home liturgical experience, although observant Jews say it wherever meals are eaten. However, they recite the *birkat hamazon* only at the conclusion of a meal that included bread. These individuals recite a shorter form of grace if they did not eat bread. Those who do not have time to recite the longer form of grace may recite this short form. The earliest text of *birkat* *hamazon* is rather short. Rabbis added to it in the geonic and medieval periods; these additions probably reflected personal preferences. The geonic period takes its name from the leader of the academy, the *gaon*, who thereby serves as community leader. The *harachaman* (the Merciful One) section may reflect the suffering of the Middle Ages. The rabbis infer the instruction for grace from the following biblical verse: "You should eat and be satisfied and bless Adonai your God for the good land which God has given you" (Deuteronomy 8:10).

Grace consists of four main blessings. The first blessing thanks God for providing food for all living creatures. The second blessing thanks God for the "good land," the redemption from Egyptian slavery, the covenant of circumcision, and the Torah. The third blessing asks God to have mercy on Israel and restore the Temple and the kingdom of David. It includes a plea that God may always sustain and support Israel. A fourth blessing thanks God for Divine goodness and includes a prayer that God may fulfill specific desires. Some suggest that this fourth blessing was added after the destruction of Betar (135 C.E.), southwest of Jerusalem. Betar was the last Israelite stronghold during the rebellion against Rome. However, Louis Finkelstein (1895–1991) argues that it may date back to the Hadrianic persecutions, approximately 132–135 C.E., corresponding to the Bar Kokha rebellion. During this period, the Roman government forbade the Jewish people from practicing many Jewish rituals, customs, and ceremonies and prevented the teaching of rabbis. This is followed by several petitions that were originally designed to suit individual needs but, like many liturgical creations, became standardized. Among Sephardic Jews there are 15 individual petitions, while Ashkenazi Jews employ only 9.

On weekdays, *birkat hamazon* is preceded by the recitation of Psalm 137, but this practice is not widely observed. The practice of reciting Psalm 126 prior to grace on Sabbaths and festivals is more common. When three or more eat together, one traditionally summons the others to say grace using a traditional formula of invitation. (See Babylonian Talmud, Berakhot 7:1–15.) This formula, known as the *zimmun*, is altered slightly among Sephardic Jews. While the Talmud suggests that as the number of people who eat together increases, the *zimmun* should become more elaborate, this practice is not widely followed. However, it is a modern practice to add the word *Elohim* (God) to the *zimmun* when there is at least a *minyan* saying grace. This probably reflects the community meals that often took place on the Sabbath. Among traditional Jews, men and women are required to use the *zimmun*.

While grace may be said in any language, it should be recited at the place where one has eaten. It is the practice of most people to leave bread on the table until the conclusion of grace. It is followed by a blessing said over a cup of wine, a practice not widely followed by liberal Jews. It has become customary to add the cup of wine only when a minimum of three is present and only on Sabbaths and festivals and other special occasions. During these special occasions, inserts are added to *birkat hamazon* that reflect the nature of the occasion.

The Conservative movement developed a shorter form of grace that primarily features the four blessings and is used in the Conservative Ramah camps. In the Reform movement, it is customary to use an abbreviated form of grace, although some Reform Jewish leaders are leading efforts to lengthen it.

Birkat hamazon takes a slightly different form and generally includes the **sheva berakhot** (seven wedding blessings) when *birkat hamazon* is recited at the meal following a wedding or during the **Seven Days of Feasting**. Following the recital of the grace after meals, the leader holds up a goblet of wine and then recites the last six wedding blessings. Then he takes a second goblet of wine and says the first blessing. Next he mixes the contents of both goblets together and gives it to both bride and groom to drink. A beverage other than wine may be used, which slightly alters the words included in the first blessing.

REFERENCES

Elbogen, Ismar. *Jewish Liturgy: A Comprehensive History*, translated by Raymond P. Scheindlin. Philadelphia: Jewish Publication Society, 1993.

Finklestein, Louis. "The *Birkat ha-Mazon*." In *Pharisaism in the Making: Selected Essays*. New York: 1972.

Schoenberg, Elliot Salo. "A Note on *Birkat Hamazon*." *Conservative Judaism* vol. 37, no. 4 (1984): 86–89.

BIRKAT KOHANIM. The priestly benediction, taken from Numbers 6:24–27 and included in the reader's repetition of the *amidah*, the central prayer in worship, recited three times a day. It is also used in many life-cycle ceremonies and forms part of the **blessing of children** on Friday evening. In some Reform congregations, the rabbi invokes a blessing on the congregation by reciting *birkat kohanim* at the conclusion of the Friday night or Saturday morning worship service. However, the popularity of this practice is waning. *Birkat kohanim* also forms the core of the ritual of **duchanen**.

As part of the Temple cult, the priests ascended a special platform to deliver the priestly benediction every morning and evening. There they pronounced the threefold priestly benediction over the people with their hands uplifted. This formulaic blessing, which the priests offered also on the Sabbath and festivals in the *musaf* services and on some fast days during the *mincha* service, may reflect an older cantation form. In the Temple, the priests uttered the tetragrammaton (the four letter name of God not to be pronounced) as part of the blessing, but those who recite it in the synagogue substitute the euphemism Adonai. It is perhaps the last remnant of the Temple cult.

REFERENCES

Elbogen, Ismar. *Jewish Liturgy: A Comprehensive History*, translated by Raymond P. Scheindlin. Philadelphia: Jewish Publication Society, 1993.

Feldman, S. S. "The blessing of the Kohenites." In *The Psychodynamics of American Jewish Life*," edited by N. Kiell. New York: Twayne Publishers, 1967, pp. 403–430.

BIRKOT HASHACHAR. Literally "blessings of the dawn," the Hebrew phrase refers to a specific set of morning blessings that are part of a daily ritual. The order of the blessings generally follows the order of things to be done on arising. Over time, rabbinic authorities gradually incorporated most of these blessings into the formal morning liturgy, because people were unable to say them privately. In the synagogue, a prayer leader could do so and worshipers could respond by saying "Amen." Thus, the phrase now refers to both. In some communities, worshipers still say the blessings at home before coming to the synagogue or recite them privately before joining in public prayer with *Pesukei D'zimra* (Verses of Song). Most congregations, however, begin their worship with the recitation of these blessings.

As the order of these blessings was never fixed by Jewish law, the order differs among prayer books. The rabbis of the Talmud suggest that individuals should recite 100 blessings each day. Thus, it is quite possible that this directive became the stimulus to make this part of the formal liturgy.

The first ritual and blessing is **netilat yadayim** (washing the hands, literally "lifting up the hands"), which refers to the act of consecration. This practice symbolizes the removal of defilement and impurity, as it did for the priest who performed this ritual act of consecration prior to beginning his daily ritual. Unlike most blessings that are to be said prior to the ritual act, this blessing is recited after washing the hands but before drying them. This blessing should be recited after dressing. However, some say it before beginning morning prayers. When recited in the synagogue, the prayer leader does not repeat it.

The recital of *asher yatzar* ("who has created") follows. This blessing praises God for the creation of the miraculous mechanisms of the body: "Praised are You, Adonai our God, Sovereign of the Universe, who was has wisely formed the human being and created many ducts and organs in him [and her]. It is well known that if but one of these is opened (when it should be closed) or if one of these is closed (when it should be open), it would be impossible to survive and stand before You. Praised are You, Adonai, who heals all flesh and does wondrous works." Traditionally, this blessing is also not said aloud by the prayer leader. However, many liberal congregations recite this prayer together aloud.

Just as *asher yatzar* praises God for the creation of body, this next blessing, *Elohai neshamah*, praises God for the creation of a soul that is pure. Because the two blessings form a unit of sorts, one should follow the other. However, because *Elohai neshamah* ("God of my soul") is listed in the Talmud as the first of a series of other blessings, it is often separated from *asher yatzar* in Ashkenazic prayer books. As this blessing is said each morning after arising from the "semi-death" of sleep, it also prefigures the restoration of the soul in the afterlife. While there is a growing interest in the afterlife among liberal Jews, resurrection of the soul was rejected by early Reform theologians. The text reads: "O my God, the soul that You placed in me in pure. You created it. You fashioned it. You breathed it into me. You preserve it in me. And one day you will take it from me and later restore it to me. As long as my soul is in me, I give thanks to You, Adonai my God and God of my ancestors, Master of all Creation, God of all souls. Praised are You, Adonai, who restores the souls to [those who sleep like the dead]."

Because each individual is enjoined to study Torah daily, the blessings that follow reflect this obligation. The first blessing is addressed to the performance of the *mitzvah* of Torah study. The second, also used when one is called up to the Torah for an ***aliyah***, is a blessing of thanksgiving, which affirms the participant's gratitude for being among those chosen to receive Torah at Sinai. Some suggest that the two blessings reflect the dual nature of Torah: oral and written law. Others, like Moses Maimonides, argue that there are actually three blessings. Thus, he suggests that the division of the first liturgical paragraph (which is technically called a "long blessing") reflects the separation of the oral law into the two sections of Mishnah and Gemara. The blessings are as follows:

Praised are You, Adonai our God, Sovereign of the Universe, who made us holy with *mitzvot* and instructed us to busy ourselves with the words (and works) of Torah. Make the words of Your Torah pleasant in our mouth, Adonai our God, and in the mouth of Your people, the House of Israel, so that we and our offspring and the offspring of Your people, the House of Israel, may all know Your Name and study Your Torah. Praised are You, Adonai, who teaches the Torah to the people Israel.

Praised are You, Adonai our God, Sovereign of the Universe, who has chosen us from among all peoples and given us the Torah. Praised are You, Adonai our God, who gives the Torah.

Because one is required to fulfill the obligation mentioned in the blessing immediately upon saying it, Torah study is included at this point in the morning ritual. As might be expected, two different traditions for this study emerged, one in Babylonia and one in the land of Israel. Thus, the custom varied as to whether worshipers said one or both. The first passage is short and immediately follows the Torah blessings. It consists of Numbers 6:24–26, which constitute the priestly blessings. This first study section also includes a selection from the Mishnah (Peah 1:1) and from the Talmud (Babylonian Talmud, Shabbat 127a). These passages emphasize Torah study and the obligation to affirm its study through explicit action as directed by the study. The second unit of study is much longer and is found at the end of this preliminary section. For this unit, the rabbis selected lengthy excerpts that deal with the laws of Temple sacrifices.

In Berakhot 60b, the Talmud lists a series of blessings to be said on arising in the morning. Each begins with the standard formula for blessing, "Praised are You, Adonai, Sovereign of the Universe." The contemporary synagogue service begins with these blessings, which, in some way, relate to daily routine. The last blessing is longer than the rest and begins with an expression of gratitude to God for "removing slumber from the eyelids." This directly relates to the washing of one's hands in the morning. But then the blessing is followed by several fervent requests for God to help the individual in the daily struggles of life.

Three controversial blessings follow. In successive order, they conclude as follows: "who has not made me a non-Jew; who has not made me a slave; and who has not made me a woman." The second blessing was placed in the liturgy instead of "who has not made me ignorant," the text recommended by Rabbi Judah in the Talmud. The traditional explanation for the conclusion of these statements focuses primarily on the ability of the individual to do God's *mitzvot*, to follow God's will. Were the individual in one of these three categories, he would be in a position to do fewer *mitzvot*. Conservative, Reform, and Reconstructionist liturgists have struggled with these statements. Most suggest restructuring the blessings so that they are stated in the positive, taking their cue from precedents already set in the liturgy, such as: "who has made me a Jew; who has made me to be free; and who has made me according to Your will." This third alternative was placed into the liturgy for women after the geonic period and adopted by liberal men in the modern period. The geonic period takes its name from the leader of the academy, the *gaon*, who thereby serves as community leader. Some offer "who has made me a man (or woman)" as an alternative to the third statement. While these three blessings are included in Ashkenazic prayer books, they are excluded from Sephardic liturgies.

Talmudic sages regularly added their own personal prayers to those fixed by tradition. These commonly became part of the liturgy. Such is the case with the personal prayer of Rabbi Judah in the Babylonian Talmud, Berakhot 16b, noted as *yehi ratzon* ("may it be Your will"), which follows the aforementioned blessings and may still be augmented by personal prayers.

The well-known biblical selection called "The *Akedah*," or the binding of Isaac, from Genesis 22:1–19 is also included in this preliminary service to emphasize the faith of our ancestors who were prepared—as we should be—to place our trust in God. This is followed by a section that focuses on a description of the sacrificial offerings. This part of the service was intended as a private substitute for the public morning service and contains some of Judaism's basic tenets. As a result, the first line of the *Shema* (and, in some cases, the entire first paragraph) is subtly included.

The preliminary service concludes with a section of Torah study (Numbers 28:1–8 and a selection of Mishnah [Zevachim 5]). These deal with the sacrifices that formed the core of the daily Temple service. While the Reform movement rejected references to the sacrificial system, much of the Jewish community resonated with the ascribed spiritual significance of these passages. Some commentators suggested that the study of the sacrifices was equivalent to bringing the sacrifices themselves. The conclusion to this section listed the hermeneutical rules for interpreting the text by Rabbi Ishmael. Other prayers that are included in the service at this point were used as a transition from the extended morning blessings to the morning service itself, the latter to be read in the synagogue.

REFERENCES

Elbogen, Ismar. *Jewish Liturgy: A Comprehensive History*, translated by Raymond P. Scheindlin. Philadelphia: Jewish Publication Society, 1993.

Heinemann, Joseph. *Prayer in the Talmud: Forms and Patterns*. Berlin: De Gruyter, 1977.

BITUL CHAMETZ. Once the *chametz* (unleavened bread) has been collected in preparation for Passover, the family gathers in order to renounce all ownership of it (*bitul chametz*) using a traditional Aramaic formula called *kol chamira*, after its first two words. This ritual is performed twice. The first time is the evening that begins on the fourteenth of Nisan, immediately after **bedikat chametz** (searching for unleavened bread). At this time, the individual annuls only the *chametz* that is not known to him or her, what was not found in the search: "which I have not seen and which I have not eliminated from my possession." The second one is performed the next day, immediately after **biur chametz** (burning of the unleavened bread). During the course of the last meal, some crumbs may have fallen—and this is after the search and the burning. Thus, this annulment includes even the *chametz* that one has seen and is aware of: "which I have seen and which I have not seen, which I have eliminated from my possession and which I have not eliminated from my possession."

REFERENCES

Goodman, Philip. *The Passover Anthology*. Philadelphia: The Jewish Publication Society of America, 1961.

Strassfeld, Michael. *The Jewish Holidays: A Guide and Commentary*. New York: Harper & Row, 1985.

Waskow, Arthur I. *Seasons of Our Joy*. New York: Summit Books, 1986.

BIUR CHAMETZ. Following the search for *chametz* prior to Passover through the process of ***bedikat chametz*** (searching for the leavened bread), it is symbolically burned (*biur chametz*). This is to take place by 10 o'clock in the morning. If the night of Passover coincides with the Sabbath, the *chametz* is searched for on Thursday evening and burned on Friday morning. In many communities, the rabbi "buys" the remaining *chametz* that might still be in one's home and then "sells" it (***mekhirat chametz***) collectively to a non-Jew. Only small quantities may be burned. Large quantities must be sold.

REFERENCES

Goodman, Philip. *The Passover Anthology*. Philadelphia: The Jewish Publication Society of America, 1961.

Strassfeld, Michael. *The Jewish Holidays: A Guide and Commentary*. New York: Harper & Row, 1985.

BLESSING OF CHILDREN. During **Friday night table rituals**, children are traditionally blessed by the father (or in some households by the mother or the mother and father). This blessing begins (for boys) with an adaptation of the text that Jacob used to bless Joseph's children, Ephraim and Menasseh, when he took them as his own (Genesis 48:20) or (for girls) with a reference to the matriarchs Sarah, Rebecca, Rachel, and Leah (see Ruth 4:11). As an optional addition to blessing of the children, ***birkat kohanim*** (Numbers 6:24–27) is usually invoked.

The blessing of children and its efficacy is attested to in various biblical narratives (see Genesis 9:26–27; 27–28:1–4; 48:13–22; 49). Historically, the blessing of children took place in the synagogue or in the home on the Sabbath, on the eve of holidays and Yom Kippur, and prior to leaving on a journey. It is deeply rooted in the medieval period. It is also recited prior to the wedding of children and on the parents' deathbed. When grandparents are still alive, it is customary to receive their blessing, as well, especially on the eve of the Day of Atonement and before the wedding ceremony. In some communities, the blessing of children by parents also takes place after **Havdalah** at the end of the Sabbath.

REFERENCE

Pearl, Chaim. "Blessing of Children." In *The Oxford Dictionary of the Jewish Religion*, edited by R. J. Zwi Werblowsky and Geoffrey Wigoder. New York: Oxford University Press, 1997.

BLOWING THE SHOFAR. The shofar is blown in the synagogue on Rosh Hashanah during the *Musaf Amidah* (central prayer during the additional service) and at the conclusion of Yom Kippur. It is also blown each morning at the conclusion of daily services during the month of Elul, which precedes Rosh Hashanah and acts as a period of preparation for it. Traditionally, when Rosh Hashanah occurs on the Sabbath, the shofar is not blown out of fear that it may be carried to someone who would teach him how to use it and then carry it to the synagogue, a practice that is prohibited on the Sabbath. This reason was added to the original prohibition. Originally, the Talmud referred to Jerusalem only as the place where the day of the new month was fixed. Other places are called "remembrance of the blowing," where the recital of the verses is sufficient. The Mishnah suggests that as long as the Temple existed in Jerusalem, the shofar was blown only there on the Sabbath, not in other places. After the destruction of the Temple, the decision of Rabbi Yochanan ben Zakkai to blow the shofar in Yavneh was augmented to include all places where a court of justice or a spiritual leader of the Jewish people resided. In most Reform synagogues, the shofar is blown on the Sabbath nonetheless, particularly because most Reform synagogues observe only one day of Rosh Hashanah.

REFERENCE

Finkle, Arthur L. *The Shofar Sounder's Reference Manual*. Los Angeles: Torah Aura Productions, 1993.

BREAKING OF THE GLASS. At the conclusion of a public wedding ceremony, a thin glass, wrapped in a napkin, is placed under the groom's foot to be smashed. Some communities place this custom after the betrothal blessings. This reflects somewhat of a controversy by authorities regarding which cup, betrothal or wedding, should be broken. As the meaning of the ritual evolved, the meaning of the broken glass changed. Some communities have erroneously chosen to use a light bulb, which is inexpensive, easily broken, and emits a great sound. Most opt for the glass used for the betrothal part of the ceremony. For superstitious reasons, some are afraid to use the glass over which the seven blessings are recited. However, many use a third glass specifically for this purpose. Some authorities trace the entire custom to two separate stories that are related together in the Talmud. They refer separately to the weddings of the children of Mar, son of Ravina and Rav Ashi. Mar broke an expensive glass in order to remind those attending the party (which he thought had gotten out of hand) that a wedding is a serious event in the life of the Jewish people. Rav Ashi acted similarly at the wedding of his children (Babylonian Talmud, Berakhot 30b–31a). However, it is clear that the Talmud, in relating these stories, is aware of the popular custom to make the weddings appear sad and therefore thwart the demons who seek to destroy happiness. At the wedding of Mar, son of Ravina, the rabbis ask Humnuna to sing. Yet, he sings a lament, "Woe unto us that we may die" (ibid.).

There is some evidence that the glass to be broken was used in the wedding blessing itself. With some wine remaining in the glass, the groom threw the wine behind him and smashed the glass against the wall in order to scare away—or even bribe—demons. Some were uncomfortable with the explanation but wanted to maintain the custom. The popularity of this wedding custom engendered reinterpretation. Some scholars argue that the breaking of the glass is part of a group of wedding customs that reflect ancient superstitions suggesting that grooms are in danger. These ancients believed that evil spirits desired the bride for themselves; thus, a variety of wedding customs emerged to mitigate the danger. People believed that demons were jealous of human happiness and sought to destroy it. In the Middle Ages, some German synagogues were built with special stones to break glasses against at the conclusion of a wedding.

While there is a wide range of interpretation of the breaking of the glass, most agree that since the beginning of the fourteenth century, it has been done as a reminder of sadness over the destruction of the Temple (and the exile from Jerusalem) even during the joy of the wedding. This explanation emerges in order to fulfill the verse,

"I will remember Jerusalem at the time of my greatest joy" (Psalm 137). In some Sephardic communities, after the groom breaks the glass, those assembled recite together the verse, "If I forget you, O Jerusalem, let my right hand lose its agility. Let my tongue cleave to the roof of my mouth, if I do not remember you; if I do not set Jerusalem as my greatest joy." Most authorities argue that the interpretation of sadness over the destruction of the Temple moved into the engagement ceremony by the sixteenth century.

Some contemporary interpreters of Jewish tradition suggest that the breaking of the glass reflects the fragility of marriage and all human relationships. Grooms break the glass to suggest to their brides that although the glass shatters, may our marriage never break. The breaking of the glass also reminds the community that although the marriage offers a taste of redemption, the world is still broken and in need of repair. Others have suggested that the breaking of the glass is reminiscent of the breaking of the first tablets on Sinai. As part of the folk culture of the people, loud noises such as the breaking of glass helped to ward off evil spirits who were said to be attracted to prosperous people and occasions. Some have suggested a vulgar connotation with regard to the successful breaking of the glass on the first attempt as a parallel to the triumphant breaking of the virginal bride's hymen, which would explain why it was considered important for the groom to break the glass. Among some liberal Jews, both bride and groom share the task of breaking of glass to dispel any sexual connotation or sexism.

Nevertheless, the breaking of the glass currently evokes joy rather than sadness. It occurs at the end of the marriage ceremony, that mythic time where the timeless is brought back into time. The custom thus encourages merriment at the *seudat mitzvah* (celebratory meal attached to a commandment) that follows. People often shout "mazel tov" after the groom breaks the glass. Because of its original connotation, most Reform Jews did not elect to include it in their weddings. However, the current generation has embraced the breaking of the glass in a spirit similar to the adopting of many other traditional rituals and customs that the movement once rejected. In some communities, the **chuppah** is lowered so that couples can enjoy a moment of privacy immediately at the conclusion of the ceremony, following the breaking of the glass.

REFERENCES

Diament, Anita. *The New Jewish Wedding*. New York: Summit Books, 1985.
Goodman, Philip and Hanna. *The Jewish Marriage Anthology*. Philadelphia: The Jewish Publication Society of America, 1965.
Lauterbach, Jacob. "The Ceremony of Breaking a Glass at Weddings." *Hebrew Union College Annual* vol. II (1925): 351–380.
Routtenberg, Lilly S., and Ruth R. Seldin. *The Jewish Wedding Book*. New York: Schocken Books, 1967.

BRIT BANOT. Literally "the covenant of daughters," the *brit banot* is a naming ceremony for girls. While this is a relatively new ceremony, the naming of daughters in a formal context is not new to Judaism. It developed as a means for providing parents of daughters with a way to celebrate their birth and enter them into the covenant with a ceremony that reflects some of the covenantal elements of ***brit milah*** (ritual circumcision). Thus, the ceremony will typically involve a recitation over wine and a formulaic ushering in of the girl into the covenant (using a feminine form of the *brit milah* blessing). The baby is also named and blessed. In place of the ritual circumcision that marks the *brit milah* ceremony, candles are often lit as a symbol of the Divine presence. There are those who have suggested the ritual piercing of the ear or, more radically, the ritual breaking of the hymen, the latter of which has gained no favor.

During the evolution of this ceremony—whose idea is more fixed than the ritual itself—other names have been used, such as *shalom nekavah* (welcome to the female); *simchat bat* (the joyful celebration of the daughter), which includes Proverbs 10:12, Numbers 24:5, and Hannah's prayer in I Samuel 2:1–10; *brit bat* (covenant for a daughter), which includes seven blessings similar to the **sheva berakhot** (seven blessings) recited at a wedding; *brit kedusha* (holy covenant), which includes Psalm 98 and is liturgically similar to *brit milah*; *brit Sarah* (covenant named for the matriarch Sarah); *brit edut* (covenant of witnessing), which reflects the image of a baby being included at the giving of Torah at Sinai; *brit rekhitzah* (covenant of cleansing), which includes the ritual washing of feet; and *brit hachayim* (covenant of life). Sephardic Jews celebrate the birth of a daughter in a naming ceremony called *zeved habat* (literally "gift of a daughter").

Variations on the *brit banot* ceremony are gaining popularity among egalitarian Conservative Jews, but it is still more commonplace in Reform and Reconstructionist congregations. Among Orthodox Jews, girls are named within the first 30 days (usually on the first Sabbath following her birth), during which time her father is honored with an ***aliyah*** to the Torah. The daughter is not present. Generally, the mother is not present either (even in the women's section where they sit separately from men during worship).

REFERENCES

Diament, Anita. *The New Jewish Baby Book; Names, Ceremonies, and Customs: A Guide for Today's Families*. Woodstock, VT: Jewish Lights Publishing, 1994.

Diament, Anita, and Howard Cooper. *Living a Jewish Life*. New York: HarperCollins, 1996.

Lauterbach, Jacob Z. *Studies in Jewish Law, Custom, and Folklore*. New York: KTAV Publishing Co., 1970, pp. 30–74.

BRIT MILAH. This refers to the covenant (*brit*) of circumcision (*milah*), which is effected through the surgical removal of the foreskin that covers the glans penis. This ritual takes place on the eighth day following the birth of a Jewish boy, although it may be delayed for medical reasons. Unlike some other rituals, it may take place on the Sabbath or on a festival, but it should not be done at night. (According to Jewish law, a child born by Caesarean section must wait until the conclusion of the Sabbath or festival.) It is performed by a ritually trained officiant called a *mohel*. The ritual usually takes place in the home of the child; however, it may also take place in the synagogue. Some hospitals formerly had rooms specifically designated for this purpose. Among some Reform families, the child is circumcised by a physician in the hospital and is then later named by the rabbi at the synagogue.

While the practice of circumcision dates back to prehistoric times as a ritual procedure, the practice can be traced in the Bible to the account of Abraham's circumcision at the age of 99. Genesis 17:11–12 reads: "Every male among you shall be circumcised. You will be circumcised in your foreskin's flesh as a sign of the covenant between you and Me. He who is eight days old shall be circumcised, every male among you throughout the generations." Circumcision confirms the Jewish status of the child. However, children who are not circumcised are also considered Jewish. Since the obligation of circumcision rests on the parents, the child who has not been circumcised is required to arrange for his own circumcision when he becomes of age.

While it is a father's duty to circumcise his son, according to Jewish law, he is permitted to transfer the obligation to a *mohel*, who acts on the father's behalf. In modern communities, the person is sanctioned by rabbinic authorities after being trained in the art of circumcision and the laws surrounding the procedure. The *mohel* also receives training in asepsis.

During the ritual, the godmother takes the baby from the mother and hands him over to the godfather, who presents the baby to the *mohel*. After briefly placing the baby in a special chair designated as the chair of Elijah (honored because of his concern over Israel forsaking the covenant with God in I Kings 19:10), the *mohel* performs the ceremony. Some synagogues have large and elaborate "chairs of Elijah" where the baby is temporarily placed just prior to the performance of the ritual. In Persia and Kurdistan, the chair of Elijah was consecrated in a ceremony called *lel ikd ill Yas*. Following the procedure, the baby is handed to the father, who says a blessing over the wine and recites a prayer for the covenant. The *mohel* then recites a prayer asking for the welfare of the baby. At the same time, the baby's name is announced.

If a child has already been circumcised but the rite of *brit milah* has not been performed, most authorities agree that a small drop of blood (called *hatafat dam brit* or *tipat dam*, literally a drop of covenantal blood) should be taken from the remaining foreskin. Either circumcision or *hatafat dam brit* (if the individual is already circumcised) is required of males who undergo the rite of conversion. However, some Reform rabbis do not insist on either requirement for adults.

The Reform movement attempted to abolish the rite of circumcision beginning in Frankfurt in 1843. While the controversy still erupts among Reform Jews—particularly when the medical community takes a position counter to the advocacy of circumcision for medical reasons—most of the controversy had died down by the 1860s. Philo was the first Jewish writer to advocate circumcision for medical reasons. Circumcision has taken on a nationalist sentiment and, consequently, is practiced even among secular Israelis. Its power is so strong that it may be the only vestige of Judaism in an assimilated family regardless of where it abides. During the Hellenistic period and during the Hadrianic persecutions, many men underwent a painful operation to reverse the procedure. Some suggest that authorities instituted the practice of tearing the foreskin away from the membrane affixing it to the glans (*periah*, laying bare the glans) to counter this practice of reversing the procedure of circumcision.

On the night preceding the circumcision, it was the custom among some communities to hold a vigil (in Yiddish *vakhnakht*, for night watch). Candles were lit; a festive meal was served; prayers were recited; and Torah was studied until midnight. Before departing, guests recited the *shema* at the bedside of the mother. The Talmud (Babylonian Talmud, Sanhedrin 32b; Bava Kamma 80a) calls this custom *yeshu'a haben* or *shevu'a haben* ("saving the son"). The notion of a ritual of any sort to take place on the evening prior to the *brit milah* probably evolved from the fact that the *mohel* checked the health of the infant on that evening. This developed to include protection against Lillith and other evil spirits: hence, the study of Torah. Among Sephardic Jews, this evening is called "midrash" because the local rabbi (*hakham*) delivers a discourse on the weekly Torah reading. The hazan chants liturgical poems and the Kaddish. In Salonika, the evening was known as *veula* and the mother stayed awake all night. And in Yemen, the mother and child were not left alone at all, and incense was burned all night in their room to ward off evil spirits.

REFERENCE

Barth, Lewis, ed. *Berit Milah in the Reform Context*. N.p.: Berit Milah Board of Reform Judaism, 1990.

Diament, Anita. *The New Jewish Baby Book; Names, Ceremonies, and Customs: A Guide for Today's Families*. Woodstock, VT: Jewish Lights Publishing, 1994.

Diament, Anita, and Howard Cooper. *Living a Jewish Life*. New York: HarperCollins, 1996.

Hoffman, Lawrence A. *Covenant of Blood*. Chicago: University of Chicago Press, 1996.

Jacob, Walter. *American Reform Responsa: Collected Responsa of the Central Conference of American Rabbis, 1889–1983*. New York: Central Conference of American Rabbis, 1983, pp. 216–237.

Lauterbach, Jacob Z. *Studies in Jewish Law, Custom, and Folklore*. New York: KTAV Publishing Co., 1970.

BUILDING A *SUKKAH* (OR DWELLING IN A *SUKKAH*). Technically, Jews are not instructed to build a *sukkah* (booth or hut) for Sukkot. Instead, they are instructed to dwell in the *sukkah*. Hence, a blessing is to be said while one sits in the *sukkah* (dwells in it) rather than after completing its construction. According to custom, as soon as Yom Kippur is concluded, one is supposed to begin the construction of the *sukkah* with at least one board. Most fulfill this custom by driving in one nail alone. The *sukkah* is a temporary structure built for the celebration of Sukkot in recognition of the temporary dwellings built by the ancient Israelites as they journeyed from Egypt to Canaan, symbolic of God's protection (see Leviticus 23:43). *Sukkot* (plural of *sukkah*) are also built in recognition of the temporary shelters built in the fields during the fall harvest season. (These booths are still used to some extent in Israel to protect harvesters from the sun during rest periods in the harvest season.) Philo of Alexandria argued that they were symbols of leisure. During the period of post-Talmudic repression, the *sukkah* evolved into a symbol of homelessness. Thus, the *sukkah* became a warning to people about the risks associated with affluence. Because the *sukkah* also became a symbol of national independence, there were times, such as during the Babylonian exile, that people refrained from building *sukkot* because they had lost their independence.

The *sukkah* is built according to specific requirements and must be exposed to the elements with a view of the stars, not in a room or under a tree. The *sukkah* must have four walls and a removable covering. This covering (*skakh*) must be made from a material that grows in the ground and has been cut from it. This roof covering should be loose enough so that the *sukkah* dweller can see the stars, but thick enough to cast a shadow in the sunlight. The *sukkah* should be decorated, and the primary custom is to decorate it with fruits and vegetables. While many synagogues build *sukkot* adjacent to the synagogue for their members, especially for those unable to do so, *sukkot* should be built next to one's home. In the classical period of the Reform movement, synagogue members did not construct these *sukkot* outside the synagogue nor adjacent to their homes. Instead, they built arbor-like structures on the *bimah* of the synagogue and decorated them with fruits and flowers.

It is the traditional obligation of males to dwell in the *sukkah*. Traditional Judaism exempts women and children. Some modified this requirement to at least one meal per day. While Reform, Conservative, and Reconstructionist Judaism exempt children, they place an equal obligation (within their respective ideological frameworks) on women.

REFERENCES

Gaster, Theodor H. *Festivals of the Jewish Year: A Modern Interpretation and Guide.* New York: William Sloane Associates, 1953.

Goodman, Philip. *The Sukkot and Simhat Torah Anthology.* Philadelphia: The Jewish Publication Society of America, 1973

Greenberg, Irving. *The Jewish Way: Living the Holidays.* New York: Summit Books, 1988.

C

CHALAKAH. From the Hebrew word for "smooth" (see Genesis 27:11), *chalakah* is a ceremony that celebrates the first time cutting of hair of boys who have reached their fourth birthday. While the ceremony is restricted to select Orthodox communities today, particularly among the Hasidim, it maintains a level of great importance in many communities, particularly among Jews from the Orient. Beginning in the sixteenth century, Jews came to Mt. Meron, the traditional burial site of Rabbi Shimon bar Yochai (second century), on the holiday Lag B'omer, which falls in the middle of the *omer* period, to commemorate the **yahrzeit** of the legendary author of the *Zohar*, Judaism's primary mystical text. On Mt. Meron, families would cut their son's hair for the first time. Family members participated by each cutting a few hairs. The ceremony concluded with a festive meal. The date for this ceremony arose because on Lag B'omer the restrictions for cutting one's hair are temporarily or fully lifted depending on one's community. By linking this haircutting to the mystical Rabbi Shimon, families raised the spiritual significance of the first haircut. The ceremony evolves from the law of *orlah*: fruit of a newly planted tree is forbidden for the first three years. The fruit of this tree is "holy, for giving praise (*hilulim*) to Adonai" (Leviticus 19:24). In the *Zohar*, the *yahzeit* of Rabbi Shimon is called *hilula deRabbi Shimon bar Yochai*.

CHALITZAH. In the case of death, a man is required to marry his brother's childless widow (*yevamah* in Hebrew), as proscribed in Deuteronomy 25: 5–6. This is called a levirate marriage (*yibbum* in Hebrew), and the surviving brother is called the *yavam* or *levir*. Should he willfully refuse to fulfill his obligation (and is not prohibited from doing so), the man is released through the ritual of *chalitzah*, as described in Deuteronomy 25: 7–10. Likewise, the ritual releases the widow to marry someone else. Over the course of time, some scholars argued that *chalitzah* took precedence over levirate marriage.

The events surrounding Judah and Tamar (Genesis 38) indicate the practice of levirate marriage in the Bible, but there is no mention of the ceremony of *chalizah*. However, in this biblical story, it appears as if the obligation rests on the father of the deceased as well as on the brother. Later the story of Ruth and Boaz reflects a levirate marriage, but this was incidental to the laws concerning the redemption of property of the deceased.

The *chalitzah* ritual begins with the appearance of the widow and the surviving brother before the *bet din* (rabbinical court) in the presence of at least ten people. The *levir* wears a special shoe on his right foot (which has come to be known as a *chalitzah* shoe). Using the Hebrew indicated in Deuteronomy 25:7, 9, the *yevamah* recites a passage that indicates the *levir*'s refusal and the *levir* similarly affirms the refusal. Next the *yevamah* removes the *chalitzah* shoe worn by the *levir*, throws it on the ground, and spits in front of him. She then recites the final passage indicated in Deuteronomy 25:9. Afterwards, those present say *chalutz ha'na'al* three times. Some argue that the *yevamah* actually spit in the *levir*'s face. As the ceremony is to be performed in public, the early practice of documenting the *chalitzah* was discontinued.

Because of the difficulties that arose from the practice of *chalitzah*, some communities required the brother(s) of a groom to document their commitment to do so at the time of their brother's marriage. In 1944, the chief rabbi of Israel decreed that the *levir* was obligated to support the levirate widow until he released her through *chalitzah*. In 1950, the chief rabbi prohibited levirate marriage and made *chalitzah* obligatory.

Although levirate marriage has been prohibited, the *chalitzah* ceremony continues in some Orthodox communities. It takes place before a rabbinical court that has been extended by additional members who do not have to be ordained rabbis. The members of the court meet to establish the parameters for the ceremony and then the *chalitzah* takes place the following morning. The *yevamah* is required to fast until the ceremony. In addition to the proscribed iteration of biblical text, additional questions are asked to insure that there are no conditions that might undermine or otherwise invalidate the ceremony. This ritual is not followed among Reform, Reconstructionist, or Conservative Jews.

REFERENCES

Elon, Menachem. *Jewish Law: History, Sources, Principles*. Philadelphia: The Jewish Publication Society of America, 1994, pp. 197–199, 389–390, 830–831, 1599–1600.
Klein, Isaac. *Responsa and Halakhic Studies*. New York: KTAV Publishing Co., 1975, pp. 13–21.

CHANUKAT HABAYIT. This term refers to the dedication of a home, the core ritual of which is the affixing of a *mezuzah*. This ritual takes its lead from the Biblical injunction, "You shall write them on the doorposts of your house and on your gates" (Deuteronomy 6:9). While the *mezuzah* is actually the doorpost itself, the term is used to refer to the handwritten parchment on which is written the first two paragraphs of the *Shema* prayer (Deuteronomy 6: 4–9; 11: 13–21), rather than the container that holds the parchment.

The *mezuzah* should be placed at every door in the home, except the bathroom, on the upper right-hand side as the person enters the room, on the upper third of the doorpost, diagonally with the upper half facing inward. A blessing is said before affixing the *mezuzah*: "Praised are You, Adonai our God, who has made us holy with *mitzvot* and instructed us to affix the *mezuzah*." Only one blessing is necessary regardless of the number of *mezuzot* being affixed.

The *mezuzah* has become more of a symbol of Jewish identity than a ritual object. When one leaves or sells one's home, the *mezuzah* is supposed to be left for the next tenant—should that tenant be Jewish. Otherwise, one should simply remove the *mezuzah* so that it may be affixed in one's new home.

CHATAN BEREISHIT. Literally "the groom of Genesis," the last ***aliyah*** before the *maftir aliyah* in the Torah service on Simchat Torah. It is an honor generally given to someone who has exhibited outstanding service to the Jewish community during the preceding year. As each day of the seven days of creation is read from the Torah, the congregation joyously responds, "and there was evening and there was morning, the first day." After each unit is concluded, the congregation joins in song, usually a wordless chant called a *niggun*. Like the **chatan Torah** in many synagogues, the *chatan bereishit* is accompanied to the Torah with singing and dancing under a **chuppah**.

REFERENCES

Chill, Abraham. *The Minhagim: The Customs and Ceremonies of Judaism, Their Origins and Rationale*. New York: Sepher-Hermon Press, 1979.
Goodman, Philip. *The Sukkot and Simhat Torah Anthology*. Philadelphia: The Jewish Publication Society of America, 1973.
Greenberg, Irving. *The Jewish Way: Living the Holidays*. New York: Summit Books, 1988.
Strassfeld, Michael. *The Jewish Holidays: A Guide and Commentary*. New York: Harper & Row, 1985.
Waskow, Arthur I. *Seasons of Our Joy: A Handbook of Jewish Festivals*. New York: Summit Books, 1986.

CHATAN TORAH. Literally "the Torah bridegroom," this **aliyah** completes the annual reading cycle of the Torah. The person honored is someone who has shown exemplary love and devotion to the Torah. However, in some traditional congregations, this honor is auctioned off. In some egalitarian settings, a *kallah* (bride) is substituted for this honor. The *chatan* is called to the Torah with a declaration of his good deeds, and a *piyyut* (liturgical poem) in praise of the Torah is read. In some synagogues, the *chatan Torah* is escorted to the *bimah* under a **chuppah** with the accompaniment of singing, dancing, and the throwing of candy and rice. In past generations in some European communities, people would light bonfires and shoot off gunpowder to add to the merriment of the "wedding." In other communities, the groom would be accompanied to the synagogue from his home with a torchlight procession. In the Levant, the guests of the groom were sprinkled with scents. The final section of Deuteronomy (33:27–34:12) is read. Then the beginning section of Genesis is read from a second scroll with the honoring of a second person as **chatan bereishit**. In some congregations, the entire scroll is unrolled so that the beginning and end stand next to each other and the congregation is literally encircled by the Torah.

This ritual may have emerged from the custom of congregations rejoicing with every newly married groom on the Sabbath after the first seven days of marriage. At that time, the groom was called to the Torah with an introduction of effusive praise and somewhat of a parody asking the permission of God and the community to call the groom forward. He was showered with candies and sent back to his seat with a Torah scroll to hold for the remainder of the service from which was read the account of the marriage of Isaac in Genesis. Thus, some congregations adapted this for their Simchat Torah celebration.

REFERENCES

Chill, Abraham. *The Minhagim: The Customs and Ceremonies of Judaism, Their Origins and Rationale*. New York: Sepher-Hermon Press, 1979.

Goodman, Philip. *The Sukkot and Simhat Torah Anthology*. Philadelphia: The Jewish Publication Society of America, 1973.

Greenberg, Irving. *The Jewish Way: Living the Holidays*. New York: Summit Books, 1988.

Strassfeld, Michael. *The Jewish Holidays: A Guide and Commentary*. New York: Harper & Row, 1985.

Waskow, Arthur I. *Seasons of Our Joy: A Handook of Jewish Festivals*. New York: Summit Books, 1986.

CHUPPAH. The term *chuppah* replaced *nisuin*, which means carried or lifted. It may derive from the fact that the bride was once carried through the streets to her new home after she was veiled by her groom (see **bedecken**). These nuptials refer to a symbolic act of intimacy that demonstrates the couple's intention to create a new home and a new life together.

From the word for canopy, the *chuppah* is the enclosure in which weddings take place. A remnant of the tribal heritage of the Jewish people, it is perhaps reflective of cohabitation as the third legal form of Jewish marriage. In earlier times, the bride was led to the groom's tent or chambers where the marriage was consummated. In the period of the Talmud, the groom's father set up a royal purple tent in the courtyard of his home where the marriage would be finalized by consummation. It was probably used to create a separate, sanctified place in the midst of the marketplace. Jacob Lauterbach argues that the use of the *chuppah*, which later gained symbolic meaning, emerged from a desire to protect and shelter the wedding couple from mortal danger, a result of the demons who sought to destroy them. During the sixteenth century, most probably in Poland, the word *chuppah* became identified with a portable canopy that was held aloft by four poles. However, it might have evolved from the covering of the bride with the groom's garment, or **tallit**, during the wedding ceremony. Thus, the word became associated with canopy more so than with any legal function. This type of *chuppah* has found its way into the ceremony by becoming part of the processional. Today, these enclosures are often decorated with flowers and vines. At other times, a large *tallit* is tied to four poles and held above the heads of the bridal couple.

In the contemporary ceremony, the groom is led to the *chuppah* before the bride and is placed there facing the rabbi eastward. Upon the arrival of the groom, the rabbi says, "*Barukh haba* (may the one who comes be blessed)." After the groom is under the *chuppah*, the rabbi recites or chants, "*Mi adir* (the One who is mighty)." Both of these texts are often sung by the cantor. Then the rabbi proceeds with the wedding ceremony. In some communities, the *chuppah* is lowered so that couples can enjoy a moment of privacy immediately at the conclusion of the ceremony, following the **breaking of the glass**.

As a result of the metaphors that abound in rabbinic literature, the *chuppah* is also used as a canopy under which a new Torah may be carried into the synagogue in a processional similar to one that may precede a wedding.

REFERENCES

Diament, Anita. *The New Jewish Wedding*. New York: Summit Books, 1985.
Goodman, Philip and Hanna. *The Jewish Marriage Anthology*. Philadelphia: The Jewish Publication Society of America, 1965.
Lauterbach, Jacob. "The Ceremony of Breaking a Glass at Weddings." *Hebrew Union College Annual* vol. II (1925), pp. 351–380.
Routtenberg, Lilly S., and Ruth R. Seldin. *The Jewish Wedding Book*. New York: Schocken Books, 1967.

CONFIRMATION. Confirmation is a rite of passage for boys and girls collectively at the age of 16 (at the conclusion of tenth grade) that takes the place in the synagogue. This ceremony was originally adapted by the Reform movement from the Lutheran Church to replace the Bar Mitzvah, and later girls were included in the ceremony (see **Bar/Bat Mitzvah**). Its purpose is to admit these new adults into the household of Israel in the presence of a congregation. It originally was used as a school graduation before it was moved into the synagogue liturgy and then applied to the holiday of Shavuot.

The ceremony usually takes place on the morning of Shavuot. In some congregations, however, the ceremony takes place on Erev Shavuot. Reflecting other trends in American Jewish ritual and worship, some congregations chose to celebrate Confirmation either on the Shabbat closest to Shavuot or even the Sunday closest to the holiday. At the 1912 annual convention of the Central Conference of American Rabbis, the national association of Reform rabbis, Joseph Krauskopf of Philadelphia suggested permanently fixing Confirmation to Simchat Torah. However, his colleagues did not adopt his resolution, which indicated both freedom of spirit and a desire for flexibility in the calendar of the ceremony itself.

Since Confirmation evolved from the Bar Mitzvah, its earliest iteration resembled the Bar Mitzvah ceremony. Innovators were motivated to develop the ceremony, because they deemed the Bar Mitzvah inadequate preparation for adult responsibilities in the nineteenth century. They also wanted to include girls in a ceremony at a time that was not ready for the consideration of a Bat Mitzvah. Some called the girls' ceremony **consecration**, particularly in the Conservative movement, but this term later took on a different meaning. Nevertheless, unlike preparation for the Bar Mitzvah, preparing for Confirmation focused primarily on the recitation of catechism-like materials, such as the Thirteen Articles of Faith by Moses Maimonides.

Developers borrowed the model for Confirmation from the Christian church, but the ceremony itself was always Jewish. While most scholars suggest that the first Confirmation probably took place in 1810 in Cassel, Westphalia, with only boys participating, Michael Meyer contends that the origin of Confirmation can be traced to Dessau in 1803. Because of early opposition to the ceremony, it was typically held in a private home or school rather than in a synagogue. Later, in Berlin in 1817, girls were included in the ceremony for the first time. As more communities adopted Confirmation, it aroused the antagonism of the traditional elements in the Jewish community, which fostered official opposition by the Prussian government in 1836 and the Bavarian government in 1838. However, this did not alter the impact or spread of Confirmation in Germany. Confirmation was introduced in Hamburg in 1818 and at the Hamburg Temple in 1822. Samuel Egers, an Orthodox rabbi, introduced Confirmation in

Brunswick in 1835, and the ceremony took place in Saxony and Hesse in 1835. French Jews celebrated Confirmation in Marseille and Bordeaux in 1841 and later in Strasbourg and Paris. At the Rabbinical Conference held in Leipzig in 1869, participants urged the adoption of Confirmation by all liberal Jews.

The ceremony really took off once it was introduced in the United States, beginning in 1846 in Congregation Anshe Chesed in New York City (which merged with Adath Jeshurun in 1874 to become Beth El). Temple Emanu-el initiated the rite in 1848, years before it absorbed Beth El.

When Confirmation was introduced into Reform congregations, the Bar Mitzvah ceremony was typically abandoned. This led to better religious school retention, which waned when the Bar Mitzvah was reintroduced. However, this was not the case in Conservative and Orthodox congregations that did not abandon the Bar Mitzvah even as they introduced Confirmation, an initiative led by lay leaders and not reluctantly accepted by clergy.

In many congregations, particularly Reform synagogues, celebrants decorate the synagogue with flowers to reflect the season of spring harvest. Participants read the Ten Commandments from the Torah and are blessed by the rabbi in front of the open ark. As there are no rigid ceremonial structures, congregations have experimented with various models for Confirmation, including musical cantatas.

Originally, Confirmation took place at the age of 13. As students stayed in high school longer and adulthood was further delayed, the age for Confirmation increased to 14, then 15. Presently, most Reform congregations observe Confirmation at age 16 (at the end of tenth grade). However, neither the age, ceremony, nor preparation are uniform in the Conservative movement. Successful confirmation programs impact significantly on post-Bar Mitzvah retention in religious school. Fearful of the negative impact on Bar/Bat Mitzvah and post-tenth grade religious school retention, congregations like Beth El in Sudbury, Massachusetts, have instituted a Siyyum Torah program at the conclusion of twelfth grade.

REFERENCES

Joselit, Jenna Weissman. *The Wonders of America: Reinventing Jewish Culture 1880–1950.* New York: Hill and Wang, 1994.
Meyer, Michael A. *Response to Modernity: A History of the Reform Movement in Judaism.* Detroit: Wayne State University Press, 1995.

CONSECRATION. This ceremony solemnizes the occasion of the beginning of formal Jewish studies for a young child. There is evidence suggesting that as early as the thirteenth century Judaism marked the first day of school for young boys. The ceremony marked the transition from the informal educational context of the home and family to the formal, institutionalized environment of the school. These early ceremonies, which may have also had resonance with **Confirmation**, generally took place on Shavuot. According to some medieval sources, the child was washed and dressed in clean clothes (as a sign of purity). He was given sweet foods (to remind him of the sweetness of Jewish study) and was covered with a coat (to protect him from the evil eye). Then he was formally accompanied to school. There he would recite the Hebrew alphabet and repeat some Biblical verses in the book of Leviticus (also known as the holiness code), which had been smeared with honey that he would lick. A formal meal, which featured hard-boiled eggs, a common symbol of rebirth and renewal, concluded the ceremony. Variations on the ceremony include a variety of magical and superstitious elements. In some cases, the teacher, rather than the father, acted as the formal escort and offered a strap, rather than honey, as a motivator for study.

The ceremony survived into the sixteenth century only in an abbreviated format, with honey on an instructional page of the Hebrew alphabet as its salient element or with the father simply asking God's blessing while giving the child a honey-coated cookie. With the ceremony no longer fixed to any one time of the year, parents were instructed to fast and offer a meal to the poor as an act of charity. Thus, young boys entered school at various times during the year. In the nineteenth century, innovations included the covering of the boy with a ***tallit***, or even a ***tefillin*** bag, rather than a coat. Cookie biscuits and almonds on which were engraved the Hebrew alphabet were given to the boys. And the father stood over the child and showered him with sweets as he recited his first lesson.

As a modern ceremony, Rabbi Samuel Wohl instituted Consecration on Sukkot shortly after his arrival at the (Reform) Reading Road Temple in Cincinnati, Ohio, in the 1920s. This temple later merged with the Plum Street Temple (K. K. Bene Jeshurun) to become the Isaac M. Wise Temple, and the newly merged congregation continued the practice. Wohl also wanted to buttress the observance and celebration of Sukkot and Simchat Torah. Some congregations celebrate Consecration on Simchat Torah. Others celebrate it on Shabbat evening during Sukkot. While it is unclear what motivated the young rabbi to introduce the specific ceremony, it may have also resulted from the conflation in Reform Judaism of Shemini Atzeret and Simchat Torah. Traditionally, children are included in the ceremony surrounding the reading of the Torah to recall the inclusion of children at the giving of Torah at Mt. Sinai, which is celebrated on Simchat Torah. The calling up of these children is called *aliyat ne'arim* or **kol hane' arim** (literally "all the children").

While the Consecration ceremony is rather simple, many congregations give children a *siddur*, or small printed Torah scroll, to mark the occasion. Sociologist Harold Himmelfarb argues that registration of the child in religious school (a ritual with no content) is the extension and replacement of the early ritual of entering the child into formal education.

REFERENCES

Cooper, John. *The Child in Jewish History*. Northvale, NJ: Jason Aronson, 1996.

Himmelfarb, Harold S., and Sergio Della Pergola, eds. *Jewish Education Worldwide: Cross-Cultural Perspectives*. New York: University Press of America, 1989.

Synagogue Histories Collection. Cincinnati, OH: American Jewish Archives.

CONVERSION. The ceremony of converting to Judaism is known as *gerut* in Hebrew, from the word for "stranger." The contemporary Reform movement coined the term "Jew-by-Choice" to refer to converts to Judaism, or proselytes, and this term has been taken on by other movements as well. It may be said that the ritual of conversion begins at the point of initial contact between the potential proselyte and a rabbi. Traditionally, the rabbi does not immediately receive the one who is interested in conversion, although the Talmud indicates that a person may be accepted as a potential proselyte once he or she indicates an awareness of the plight of the Jewish people (Babylonian Talmud, Yevamot 47a). However, the practice of initially turning people away is not followed by most non-Orthodox and some Orthodox rabbis. It is clear that circumcision was the only Biblical requirement for conversion for males. Women converted through marriage to Jewish men. In the period of the Temple, a convert was required to sacrifice a burnt offering.

Today, the potential convert is schooled in the area of basic Jewish practice and knowledge. It is common practice for the potential convert to take a course of study that may be sponsored by a religious movement and cooperatively taught by a group of rabbis and teachers. The course is then followed by **brit milah** or *hatafat dam* for males and immersion in the mikvah (ritual bath) for both males and females. Immersion was probably initially introduced as a result of the state of ritual uncleanliness of non-Jews, a practice dating from at least the first century of the Common Era. In cases where a mikvah is not available, natural bodies of water are also used. When a natural body of water is not available, the Conservative movement permits the use of a swimming pool (adapted for this purpose). The blessing concerning immersion is said after the immersion has taken place (rather than before the ritual act as is usually the case). Many Reform rabbis do not require *brit milah*, *hatafat dam*, or immersion. In the past, the *bet din* (rabbinical court) validated each of the steps of the conversion process. However, today the convert is required to come before a *bet din* only after the prior requirements have been met. The *bet din* is generally an ad hoc institution (in the non-Orthodox community) set up for this individual purpose alone and comprised of three rabbis. Some Reform rabbis perform the conversion in the context of a synagogue service, at which time the convert is given the Torah to hold and asked to recite the initial lines of the *Shema*. Other Reform rabbis perform the conversion in a similar fashion, witnessed by friends and relatives in a private ceremony. During the conversion, the individual is given a Hebrew name with the patronymic "ben Avraham" (son of Abraham) or "bat Avraham" (daughter of Abraham). The Reform, Reconstructionist, and egalitarian Conservative Jews add "v'Sarah" (and Sarah).

Regardless of the specific movement, adopted children not born of Jewish parents must undergo conversion. Should a minor be converted by his or her parents, when that child comes of age, he or she is permitted to annul the conversion. However, this option must be initiated immediately or it is no longer valid.

In 1893, the Central Conference of American Rabbis abolished the requirement of any ritual for conversion, including circumcision. However, most Reform rabbis require *brit milah*. An in-depth discussion concerning the issue of immersion in the ritual bath was never undertaken by liberal authorities and the practice fell into disuse. Nevertheless, the trend appears to be in support of these requirements in addition to the appearance before a *bet din*.

REFERENCES

Epstein, Lawrence J., ed. *Readings in Conversion to Judaism*. Northvale, NJ: Jason Aronson, Inc., 1995.

Jacob, Walter, and Moshe Zemer, eds. *Conversion to Judaism in Jewish Law: Essays and Responsa*. Tel Aviv and Pittsburgh: Rodef Shalom Press, 1994.

D

DEVAR TORAH. A *devar Torah* literally refers to a "word of Torah" and means an explanation or explication of a Torah text. In Yiddish, it is called a *vort* (word). While historically there were contexts in which a *devar Torah* was expected (such as by a groom prior to his wedding), people presented *divrei Torah* (plural) at various occasions. In the contemporary community, women are also either sharing in the teaching with the groom (in liberal communities) or offering *divrei Torah* to other women in places such as the bridal room (in the Orthodox community). In the Orthodox community, the groom offers his *devar Torah* at the party (generally referred to as a *tish*) that precedes the wedding. However, it is customary for his friends to heckle him during the presentation.

In the context of the synagogue service, extensive *divrei Torah* were only given twice a year: on the Sabbath before Pesach and on the Sabbath between Rosh Hashanah and Yom Kippur. When the Reform movement truncated the liturgy in Europe in the nineteenth century, the sermon became central to the service. Thus, rabbinic preachers lengthened the sermon and spoke on topics that were not necessarily related to the Torah text. This trend spread to the other movements as well. However, sermons have fallen out of vogue in recent years throughout the movements and have been replaced by *divrei Torah* and Torah discussions.

REFERENCE

Saperstein, Marc. *Jewish Preaching, 1200–1800: An Anthology*. New Haven: Yale University Press, 1992.

DIVORCE. While there are legal aspects to a divorce, the ritual component focuses on the delivery of a *get* (document of release) by a husband to a wife. This document was formerly known as a *sefer keritut* (letter of severance). In most countries outside of Israel, the *get* follows the civil divorce and only consummates the separation. In Orthodox and Conservative communities the *get* is required for remarriage. However, most Reform rabbis accept a civil divorce in its stead, though some have suggested the delivery of a modified document (*seder peridah*).

The *get*, which predates the **ketubah** (marriage certificate), became important because of the question of *mamzerut* (bastard status). This meant that the child of a woman "married" a second time (without a *get*) or with someone who was forbidden by Jewish law placed the child's status in jeopardy.

According to the norms of Jewish law, the grounds for divorce may be divided into four general categories:

1. Cases of mutual consent where both parties agree to the divorce;
2. Cases where the husband sues for divorce, claiming that the wife is the guilty party;
3. Cases where the wife petitions for divorce, and the husband, as the guilty party, is compelled by the court to grant her a divorce; and
4. Cases of divorce enforced by the court without the petition of either party.

These categories may be further subdivided according to the numerous stipulations of Jewish law. However, while traditional Jewish law suggests that only a husband may grant a divorce to a wife and that he may do so without her consent, this generally is no longer followed.

During the divorce proceedings, an individual rabbi or a *bet din* (ad hoc rabbinical court of three rabbis) issues a *get*, which is prepared by a *sofer* (scribe) and may be written on white paper (rather than parchment). However, the woman may technically write it herself, something that is a very rare occurrence. Witnesses are required during the actual deliverance of the *get*; they must have no interest in the proceedings and no relationship with the individuals involved. These proceedings may only take place when courts are permitted to be in session. Thus, they may not take place at night, on the Sabbath or festivals, on Fridays or on days before the advent of festivals.

The rabbi asks a series of questions to the husband related to his coming there of his own free will. Then the scribe makes a "gift" of the writing materials, which the husband accepts. The husband lifts them up and makes a statement to the witnesses so that they may see him present the writing materials to the scribe authorizing him to prepare the *get*. Then the husband asks each witness to sign the *get*. They agree to do so and make a distinguishing mark on the *get*. After the *get* has been prepared and the ink has dried, the witnesses sign it and say aloud that they are signing it.

The rabbi next asks the *sofer* whether that is the *get* that he prepared and outlines a series of questions regarding its preparation. The rabbi questions the witnesses about their witnessing and about their signatures. Then the rabbi repeats a series of questions from the beginning of the procedure that affirms the *sofer*'s participation without coercion. Finally, the rabbi asks the woman to remove all jewelry from her hands and then to open them to receive the *get*. The *sofer* folds the *get* and gives it to the rabbi, who gives it to the woman. She accepts it, lifts up her hands, walks a short distance, then returns to the rabbi. The rabbi reads the *get* again and gets confirmation from the *sofer* and witnesses again. The rabbi then cuts the four corners of the *get*. This process dissolves the marriage.

At the Paris Sanhedrin in 1806, the decision of those assembled was that no religious divorce would be granted unless a valid civil divorce preceded. Most modern Jewish communities have adopted this practice.

REFERENCES

Amram, David W. *The Jewish Laws of Divorce according to Jewish Law and Talmud*. New York: Hermon Press, 1968.

Bulka, Reuven. *Jewish Divorce Ethics*. Ogdensburg, NY: Ivy League Press, 1992.

Haut, Irwin. " 'The Altar Weeps': Divorce in Jewish Law." In *Celebration and Renewal*, edited by Rela Geffen Monson. Philadelphia: The Jewish Publication Society of America, 1993.

Mielziner, Moses. *Jewish Law of Marriage and Divorce in Ancient and Modern Times*. Cincinnati: Bloch Publishing Co., 1884 (2nd ed., rev. New York: Bloch Publishing Co., 1901).

Riskin, Shlomo. *Women and Jewish Divorce*. Hoboken, NJ: KTAV Publishing Co., 1989.

DUCHANEN. As part of the Temple cult, the priests ascended a special platform (called a *duchan*; hence is derived the Yiddish expression *duchanen*, "to deliver the priestly benediction") every morning and evening. There they pronounced the threefold priestly benediction (***birkat kohanim*** in Hebrew) from Numbers 6: 24–26 over the people with their hands raised in a special way. This formulaic blessing, which the priests offered also on the Sabbath and festivals in the *musaf* services and on some fast days during the *mincha* (afternoon) service, may reflect an older cantation form. (The *musaf*, or additional worship service, reflects the additional sacrifice brought to the Temple on Shabbat and holidays.) In the Temple, the priests uttered the tetragrammaton (four letter name of God that was only pronounced once a year) as part of the blessing, but those who recite it in the synagogue substitute the euphemism Adonai (which literally means Lord) and apply the Hebrew vowels of Adonai to the tetragrammaton so that the reader will not make a mistake when reading. It is perhaps the last remnant of the Temple cult, preserved in the last blessing of the *Amidah*, the core prayer in Jewish worship.

Duchanen is the obligation of every adult *Kohane* (descendant of the priestly class) unless he is in mourning or is unable to do so because of physical disability. In apologizing for these restrictions, scholars argued that it distracted the congregants. A descendant of the priesthood is also exempt if he killed someone, committed idolatry, married a woman forbidden to him, or is intoxicated. The blessing takes place only in public worship when a *minyan* is assembled.

In order to recite the blessing, the priests prepare themselves by removing their shoes and ritually washing their hands, assisted by the Levites. After the *chazan* introduces the blessing during the reader's repetition of the *Amidah*, the priests turn toward the congregation and pronounce the blessing for the performance of this *mitzvah* (commandment). It is the custom in Israel for a member of the congregation to call out for the priests to come forward. Then the *chazan* says each word of the priestly benediction, which the priests then repeat. In all cases, the priests recite the words with prayer shawls drawn over their heads. They stretch their hands out at shoulder height with their palms facing forward. Each priest holds his hands touching at the thumbs, with the first two fingers of each hand separated from the other (spread like a fan of sorts). It is customary for the congregants not to look at the priests while they perform the task of blessing. As the priests recite each line of blessing, the congregation responds by saying, "Amen." However, if the *chazan* recites the blessing instead of the priests, the congregation responds after each line by saying in Hebrew, *"Ken yihi ratzon"* (May it be Your will).

It is the general Ashkenazic custom of performing *duchanen* only on the High Holidays and during the three pilgrimage festivals. In Israel, the blessing is performed every Shabbat during the morning and additional *musaf* service. However, in Jerusalem it customarily takes place every day.

While Reform and Reconstructionist congregations have eliminated this practice and often replace it with a rabbi's benediction at the end of a worship service following a Protestant model, some Conservative and Reconstructionist congregations maintain the practice of *duchanen* on the High Holidays.

REFERENCES

Elbogen, Ismar. *Jewish Liturgy: A Comprehensive History*, translated by Raymond P. Scheindlin. Philadelphia: Jewish Publication Society, 1993.

Feldman, S. S. "The Blessing of the Kohenites." In *The Psychodynamics of American Jewish Life*," edited by Norman Kiell. New York: 1967, pp. 403–430.

E

ELIJAH'S CUP. As part of the table setting for the *seder* during Passover a fifth cup of wine is filled and set aside for the prophet Elijah, who is designated to herald the coming of the Messiah. This cup gave rise to the notion of Elijah's invisible presence at the *seder*. Because there is a dispute in the Talmud regarding whether there should be four or five cups of wine at the *seder*, the rabbis made the decision to wait until Elijah comes to resolve the conflict. Thus, the fifth cup came to be known as Elijah's cup. While waiting in hopeful anticipation of Elijah's arrival, celebrants open the door to welcome him. This custom probably developed during the Inquisition when Jews opened the door to check to see if there were any spies outside before they returned to the second part of the *seder*. Perhaps it was a way to fend off the "blood libel" by showing people that there was no child being sacrificed inside. Once the door is opened, some families then pour out the wine into the cups around the *seder* table. Others pour a little wine from their cup into Elijah's as a way of indicating that we all have a role in bringing the Messiah. However, it is clear that the tradition does not encourage drinking this wine with a separate blessing. Some scholars have suggested that people should, indeed, do this, being the generation that has been brought back to the land of Israel through the establishment of the modern state. Others play games with the wine in Elijah's cup by disposing of it in creative ways while the children open the door for Elijah.

REFERENCE

Wiener, Aharon. *The Prophet Elijah in the Development of Judaism.* Boston: Routledge & K. Paul, 1978.

F

FAST OF THE FIRSTBORN. Called *taanit bekhorim* in Hebrew, this ritual is performed in appreciation to God for sparing the lives of the firstborn of Israel at a time when the firstborn of Egypt were killed during the last plague. It reflects the plethora of primogeniture rules that no longer concern us in the modern world. Firstborn male children are required to fast until nightfall on the day before Passover. Jewish law obligates only the child who is the firstborn of the mother and the firstborn of the father. While it is not a practice widely followed, a parent can fast on behalf of a minor child. However, most families simply wait until the child comes of age. Some traditional authorities require women to fast as well, even though they will not acquire the status of the firstborn. Some individuals who are not firstborn choose to fast in order to heighten the taste of *matzah* at the *seder*. In many communities, this fast is obviated by the public reading and explanation of the concluding passage of Talmud (called a *siyyum*) with one who is, indeed, in the process of concluding the study of a particular tractate of Talmud. As eating after such an occasion is considered to be a *seudat mitzvah* (festive meal that accompanies the fulfilling of a *mitzvah* obligation), the firstborn who participate in such an occasion may join the festivities. Thus, this cancels or concludes the fast. The participation in any *seudat mitzvah*, such as one following a **brit milah**, **Bar/Bat Mitzvah**, or wedding, works the same way. If this day falls on a Sabbath, then it takes place on the preceding Thursday.

REFERENCES

Goodman, Philip. *The Passover Anthology*. Philadelphia: The Jewish Publication Society of America, 1993.

Gottlieb, Nathan. *A Jewish Child is Born: The History and Ritual of Circumcision, Redemption of the Firstborn, Adoption, Conversion, and Giving of Names*. New York: Bloch Publishing Co., 1960.

Greenberg, Irving. *The Jewish Way: Living the Holidays*. New York: Summit Books, 1988.

Ki Tov, Eliyahu. *The Book of Our Heritage*. New York: Feldheim, 1997, pp. 205–207.

FRIDAY NIGHT TABLE RITUALS. The Sabbath is ushered in with the lighting of Sabbath candles (***hadlakat hanerot***) 18 minutes prior to sunset on Friday evening. This begins the process of receiving the Sabbath, which is called ***kabbalat Shabbat***. However, many Reform Jews light candles whenever they sit down to dinner on Friday evening. *Kabbalat Shabbat* is a mystical set of prayers comprised of six introductory psalms that reflect the six days of creation plus a kingship motif. Following the psalms is the hymn *lecha dodi*, which focuses on Shabbat and the matching queenship motif. *Kabbalat Shabbat* concludes with the psalm for the seventh day.

In many traditional families, candles are lit at home by the women in the family, while the men are ushering in the Sabbath with the evening service at the local synagogue. In those families where the candles have already been lit, Friday night table rituals begin with the singing of the hymn *Shalom Aleikhem*, a late composition that is sung by Ashkenazi Jews to invite angels to join them throughout the Sabbath, an idea based on the Babylonian Talmud, Shabbat 119a. In traditional neighborhoods, this hymn is often sung as families walk back from the synagogue. In many families, the singing of this hymn precedes the lighting of the candles. Traditionally, this is followed by the **blessing of children** by the father (or in some households by the mother or the mother and father).

It is the tradition of some families to bless the children following the recitation of Proverbs 31: 10–31, often called "A Woman of Valor," taken from the first line of the selected verse, which is spoken by the husband in honor of his wife. In some families, the wife responds with either a regendered version of the text or an alternative text.

After the blessing of children comes the recitation of **kiddush**, which is used to consecrate the Sabbath and is said while standing over an overflowing cup of wine generally held in the palm of the hand with five fingers curled upward like a five-petaled rose. Grape juice may be used instead. If wine or juice is not available, *kiddush* may be said over bread. (One simply replaces the blessing for the wine in the *kiddush* with **hamotzi**, the blessing for bread.) While it is the tradition of some to wash the hands ritually (**netilat yadayim**) prior to *kiddush*, most people wash following *kiddush* but before saying *hamotzi*. The *challah* bread, which is left covered until this point, is now uncovered. As a result of or in anticipation of these table rituals, the Sabbath table has been symbolically transformed into the altar of the ancient Temple in Jerusalem. Hence, most people do not cut the *challah* with a knife following the blessing called *hamotzi*. Rather, they tear it. Two *challahs* are used, reminiscent of the two portions of manna that were collected in the wilderness on Fridays during the journey of the Israelites from Egypt to Canaan. The *challah* is slightly salted (as would be a sacrifice) and then torn apart by hand. It is prohibited to even have a knife near the *challah* because knives, as implements of war, were not permitted near the Temple altar. Then dinner is served, often interspersed with the singing of Sabbath table songs called *zemirot*.

The meal concludes with the singing of **birkat hamazon**, the grace after meals. But because it is Shabbat, people do not rush away from the table. Instead, they linger and sing additional Sabbath songs together. Various community and family customs have developed with regard to Sabbath table rituals, some of which are followed also on Saturday at lunch, which is considered the second meal.

REFERENCES

Elbogen, Ismar. *Jewish Liturgy: A Comprehensive History*, translated by Raymond P. Scheindlin. Philadelphia: Jewish Publication Society, 1993.

Hammer, Reuven. *Entering Jewish Prayer: A Guide to Personal Practices and the Worship Service*. New York: Schocken Books, 1994.

G

GELILAH. From the Hebrew "to roll," *gelilah* refers to the dressing of the Torah following its public reading, after it has been raised. The individual who is to do the rolling is called to the *bimah* as with any other Torah honor. It is the custom of some congregations to call this person by the task rather than by the Hebrew name. Ashkenazic congregations raise the Torah (*hagbah*) after it is read and thus call the person for this honor at the same time as the person called for *gelilah*. In contrast, Sephardic congregations raise the Torah prior to its reading; thus, the person responsible to roll the Torah is called separately. (Ashkenazi refers to communities that originally derive from Germany, while Sephardic refers to communities that have their origin in Spain.)

REFERENCES

Elbogen, Ismar. *Jewish Liturgy; A Comprehensive History*, translated by Raymond P. Scheindlin. Philadelphia: Jewish Publication Society, 1993.

Klein, Isaac. *A Guide to Jewish Religious Practice*. New York: The Jewish Theological Seminary of America, 1979.

H

HADLAKAT HANEROT. Literally "the lighting of candles," *hadalakat hanerot* takes place on Sabbath and holidays. In Yiddish the ritual is referred to as *benchen licht* (blessing of the candles); thus, it is sometimes referred to similarly in Hebrew as *birkot hanerot* (blessings of the candles). The ritual includes a specific blessing, generally tailored for the occasion. The custom of lighting the Sabbath light originates in the Mishnah (Shabbat 2:6–7) where only one light is mentioned. Some suggest that as light and joy are used as synonyms in the Bible (Psalm 97:11 and Esther 8:16), the rabbis wanted the light to be kindled in an effort to emphasize the joy of the Sabbath. Later, the custom of lighting two lamps, particularly among the wealthy, evolved to reflect the two occasions in the Torah in which the commandment to observe the Sabbath is mentioned (Exodus 20:8 and Deuteronomy 5:12). During more prosperous times, the custom to light a candle for each member of the family or each child in the family arose.

Unless women are not present, it is customary on Sabbath and holidays for women to light the candles, this being one of their three primary obligations. However, the responsibility for this commandment rests with men as well as women. Furthermore, men and women light candles on Hanukkah. Among liberal Jews, nothing prevents men from lighting candles, but in family contexts, the ritual tends to fall to women. As an analog, men light the **havdalah** candle at the end of the Sabbath.

While the lighting of candles is a home ritual, most Reform congregations light candles in the synagogue prior to or during late Friday night or festival worship, presumably as an analog to the reciting of *kiddush* in the synagogue, which was instituted for the benefit of travelers or for those who were unable to do so at home. However, it was a custom revived from ancient times when candles were lit following the afternoon service in the synagogue. Some Conservative congregations also make *kiddush* in the synagogue following services, even when services are held late in the evening.

While the candles may be lit in a variety of places in the house, it is customary to light them at the table where the candle holders should remain for the entire Sabbath or holiday period even after the candles have burned down. Some authorities permit the moving of the candles after they have been burning for a short time.

It is the traditional practice to pronounce a blessing prior to the lighting of the candles. However, many Reform congregations light the candles prior to reciting the blessing. This blessing is not found in the Talmud. It first appears in the ninth-century prayer book of Saadia Gaon (882–942). After the candles have been lit, it is traditional to close one's eyes and encircle the candles three times with one's hands and arms to focus attention and bring the light of Shabbat fully into oneself.

Hadlakat Hanerot—Hanukkah

Hanukkah candles are lit in a specially designated candelabra referred to as a *chanukiyah*. This contains nine candle holders or oil containers, eight of which are designated one for each day of Hanukkah and the ninth is to be used to light the others. The candles are placed in the *chanukiyah* one for each night in ascending order from the right to the left. And the candles are lit from the left to the right, starting with the candle designated for any one particular night during the eight. The *chanukiyah* is to be placed in a window in order to "publicize the miracle" of Hanukkah. No work is to be done while the candles are burning; the candles must burn for at least a half hour. There is no requirement as to the nature of the material used for the *chanukiyah*. However, traditional Jewish law requires that each candle holder should be of the same height and that the ninth holder (called the *shamash*, or helper) must be raised or separate from the rest. Reform rabbis generally accept contemporary *chanukiyot* as fitting for use. While there are some objections to gas and electric *chanukiyot*, they are acceptable under Jewish law.

Two blessings are required upon lighting the candles each night. The first blessing is a standard candle lighting, blessing adjusted for Hanukkah. The second blessing takes note of the miracles: "in this season in years past." The *shehechiyanu* blessing is added on the first night only.

REFERENCES

Birnbaum, Philip. *A Book of Jewish Concepts*. New York: Hebrew Publishing Co., 1975.

Greenberg, Irving. *The Jewish Way: Living the Holidays*. New York: Touchstone, 1988.

Olitzky, Kerry M. *Eight Nights, Eight Lights*. Los Angeles: Alef Design Group, 1996.

Wolfson, Ron. *The Shabbat Seder*. Woodstock, VT: Jewish Lights Publishing, 1996.

HAFTARAH. The *haftarah* is a selection from the prophets that is read on the Sabbath and holidays following the reading of the Torah. Individual *haftarah* readings are somehow (even if loosely) connected to a theme established by the Torah reading. The person honored with the reading of the *haftarah* is given the final or *maftir* **aliyah** during the reading of the Torah. The reader recites two short blessings prior to the reading of the *haftarah* and a series of longer blessings following its conclusion. While there are those who believe that the *haftarah* was introduced during the time of Roman persecution when the Jewish people were prohibited from reading the Torah, more likely it was introduced as a pedagogic measure to emphasize the lesson of the weekly Torah reading. In many Reform synagogues, the *haftarah* is read exclusively in English, and in some Reform synagogues, it is not read at all. As the *haftarah* selection was rather loose, the Ashkenazic community selected a different group of readings than did the members of the Sephardic community. (Ashkenazi refers to communities that originally derive from Germany, while members of the Sephardic community have their ancestral origins in Spain.)

REFERENCE

Plaut, W. Gunther, ed. *The Haftarah Commentary*. New York: Union of American Hebrew Congregations, 1996.

HAGBAH. This is the act of lifting the Torah after it has been publicly read in the synagogue in the midst of worship in Ashkenazic congregations. In anticipation of the raising of the Torah, the congregation stands. This follows the logic that as individuals are required to stand in the presence of those learned in Torah (as Leviticus 19:32 is understood), then surely individuals should stand before the Torah itself (Babylonian Talmud, Kiddushin 33b). As the Torah is raised, the congregation chants a text that includes the verse "'This is the Torah which Moses placed before the Israelites' (Deuteronomy 4:44) from the mouth of God through the hand of Moses." During this time, it is customary to point to the Torah with the little finger of the right hand, with the finger loosely wrapped in a *tzitzit* fringe. Among some communities, the eyes are touched as well. According to Maimonides, the Torah should be opened while it is raised to expose at least three columns of text and one binding. Afterwards, the Torah is rerolled and wrapped as part of **gelilah**.

During the intertestamental period, the *hagbah* ritual took place prior to the reading of the Torah to insure the participants that a sectarian group had not replaced the Torah. In Sephardic ritual, the Torah is still raised prior to its reading rather than after.

The individual who is to raise the Torah is called to the *bimah* as with any other Torah honor. It is the custom of some congregations to call this person by the task rather than by his Hebrew name. In Ashkenazic congregations, the person is called along with the individual who is called for *gelilah*. Among Sephardic Jews, the person responsible to roll the Torah is called separately, as his responsibility takes place at a different time in the service.

On Simchat Torah, *hagbah* is done in a special fashion. The person lifts his hands so that when the scroll is lifted, it is reversed and facing the congregation. This symbolizes the turning back of the Torah to its beginning as a way of marking this event on the holiday of Simchat Torah. It also reflects the text from *Pirke Avot*, "Turn it [the Torah] over and over, for everything is in it."

REFERENCES

Elbogen, Ismar. *Jewish Liturgy: A Comprehensive History*, translated by Raymond P. Scheindlin. Philadelphia: Jewish Publication Society, 1993.

Jacobson, Bernhard S. *The Sabbath Service*. Tel Aviv: Sinai Publishing, 1981, pp. 268–270.

Klein, Isaac. *A Guide to Jewish Religious Practice*. New York: The Jewish Theological Seminary of America, 1979.

HAKAFOT. *Hakafot* is the circuit, or processional, ritual that generally takes place prior to and after the public reading of the Torah. Similar processionals take place during the year during the festival of Sukkot and on Hoshanah Rabbah when the Ark is open and the Torah remains on the *bimah* with someone holding it. The Torah processional ritual probably developed as congregations grew in size so that the Torah could no longer simply be removed from the ark and read. The person carrying the Torah (with the Torah leaning on the right shoulder) should lead the rest of those in the processional. The processional takes place in a counterclockwise direction prior to the reading of the Torah and a clockwise direction following its reading. In many congregations, worshipers form rows in the aisles of the synagogue so that the Torah can pass among them. One follows the direction of the Torah by turning the body as it moves through the congregation so that one never is in a position to turn one's back on the Torah. As the Torah approaches, one should step toward it. It is customary to kiss the Torah by touching a prayer book or *tzitzit* to it and then kissing the prayer book or *tzitzit*. If one cannot get to the Torah, it is customary to bow as it approaches.

Some congregations make a processional circuit with the Torah only before it is read. Many Reform congregations do not perform *hakafot* at all. Among Orthodox Jews, the processional only takes place among men. In nonegalitarian Conservative congregations, the processional may take place among women, but men carry the Torah. Among other Conservative congregations, as well as Reform and Reconstructionist synagogues, men and women share the honors equally.

On Simchat Torah, *hakafot* take a different form. Seven separate circuits are led by different groups of people and interspersed with dancing. The Torah is read following the last circuit.

REFERENCE

Isaacs, Ronald. *Every Person's Sukkot, Shemini Atzeret, and Simchat Torah.* Northvale, NJ: Jason Aronson, 1999.

HAMOTZI. Literally "the One who brings forth," the *hamotzi* blessing to God as the One who brings forth bread from the earth. This blessing is used prior to eating bread, and bread represents all the food that is about to be eaten. The textual origin for this blessing is in the Mishnah (Berakot 6:1) and both Talmuds (Babylonian Talmud, Berakhot 38a–b, Jerusalem Talmud 6:1). The biblical reference emerges from the psalmist (104:14) who wrote, "You make the grass grow for the cattle and herbage for human labor, that the human may get food out of the earth (*l'hotzi lechem min ha-aretz*)." When *challah* (braided egg twist) is eaten on Shabbat or holidays (shaped in round loaves), two loaves are used to symbolize the double portion of manna given to the Israelites during their desert journey. The bread is to be held one on top of another. And because the dinner table symbolizes the sacrificial altar of the ancient temple, the bread is slightly salted (as if it were a sacrifice). One washes one's hands ritually with a specific blessing. Then, without any additional communication (which would interfere with the act referenced by the blessing), the individual recites the *hamotzi* blessing. The bread is separated by tearing. As "the host breaks the bread" (Babylonian Talmud, Berakhot 46a), pre-sliced bread is not used. Because knives—as weapons of war—were not allowed on the Temple altar, they are prohibited from being used for the initial cut of the *challah* as well.

REFERENCES

Elbogen, Ismar. *Jewish Liturgy: A Comprehensive History*, translated by Raymond P. Scheindlin. Philadelphia: Jewish Publication Society, 1993.

Klein, Isaac. *A Guide to Jewish Religious Practice*. New York: The Jewish Theological Seminary of America, 1979.

HAVDALAH. The ceremony of separation that distinguishes Shabbat from the rest of the week, *havdalah* is also used to distinguish festivals from regular time. In both cases, the ritual is used to separate the sacred from the ordinary days of the week. Rabbinic scholars consider the ritual among one of the oldest as it is mentioned in the Babylonian Talmud (Berakhot 33a). While some suggest that it is derived from the Torah, the ritual was originally part of the *amidah*. The early authorities ruled that the ritual should be recited over a cup of wine. Thus, the rabbis of the Jerusalem Talmud (Berakhot 5:2) argue that the ceremony was transferred to a cup of wine "for the benefit of the children," and was instituted simultaneously during the *amidah* and in a separate ceremony. During the medieval period, the custom developed that the ritual should be recited over a cup of wine in the synagogue as well.

The text for the ceremony developed over a long period of time.

Ashkenazi authorities added verses (Isaiah 12:2–3) to the beginning of the ceremony as a good omen. (Ashkenazi refers to communities which originally derive from Germany.) This introduction is followed by three blessings over wine, a braided multiwicked candle, and spices. While the schools of Hillel and Shammai differed over the texts of these blessings and their order (see Berakhot 8:5), Rabbi Judah Hanasi said the two additional blessings over the cup of wine "for the benefit of the household" (Pesachim 54a). Following the ritual, it is customary to chant special hymns and songs. Among the most popular is Elijah the prophet in Hebrew (*Eliyahu Hanavi*).

Many explanations have been offered for the symbolic ritual elements that are part of *havdalah*. Wine reflects the obligation to make *havdalah*, just as one makes *kiddush* over a cup of wine. The candle is used to emphasize that the Sabbath is over and work is permitted once again. There is a great deal of debate over the ritual meaning of the spices. Some suggest that it is to compensate (or even revive) the individual over the loss of the additional soul that accompanies the individual throughout Shabbat. The final blessing, which makes the distinction between the Sabbath and the other days of the week, originally mentioned only the distinction between the Sabbath day and the rest of the week. As a result of the addition of other distinctions by individuals, people began to add those distinctions to the blessing. Then the set of distinctions became standard to the blessing. The Talmud suggests that if one is going to add distinctions, then no less than three must be added and no more than seven are permitted to be added.

A variety of customs have evolved concerning the ritual of *havdalah*. Some individuals pour the wine onto the ground as an omen for blessing. Some overfill the cup. Others touch to the eyes the last drop of wine in the cup and extinguish the flame with the remaining drops of wine. Most look at their fingertips (or the lines in their hands) in the reflected light of the candle. When a festival follows the Sabbath, *havdalah* is contained in the blessing for the day in connection with **kiddush**. When *havdalah* is followed by a regular day, the ritual is recited without candle or spices.

While Orthodox and Conservative Jews continued to practice this ritual, the ceremony of *havdalah* found its way back into the Reform movement primarily through its summer camps for children as *havdalah* is often made outdoors.

REFERENCES

Greenberg, Irving. *The Jewish Way: Living the Holidays.* New York: Touchstone, 1988.

Yehuda, Zvi A. "The Ritual and the Concept of *Havalah*." *Judaism* vol. 43, no. 1 (1994): 78–86.

HESPED. A eulogy that is given to honor the memory of the deceased, the *hesped* tradition emerges from a variety of contexts in the Bible (see II Samuel 1:12, for example). It is a religious duty that stems from the directive to "love one's neighbor as oneself" (Shulkhan Aruch, Yoreh Deah 344:1). A eulogy emphasizes the virtues of the deceased, but Jewish law advises the one giving the eulogy to avoid excessive praise. The rabbis of Talmud debated whether the purpose of the eulogy was to pay tribute to the family of the deceased or to honor the deceased and decided on the latter (Babylonian Talmud, Sanhedrin 46b–4a). In some cases, such as during the Roman occupation of Jerusalem, community leaders did not offer eulogies for martyrs out of fear of repercussions. In the ancient Babylonian academies, teachers offered eulogies for those rabbis who had died during particular seasons, although Jewish law stipulates that the eulogy should be pronounced within the seven-day period following the death of an individual. Later, in Central and Eastern Europe, communities prepared eulogies on Adar 7 for rabbis who died during the prior year. In some communities, eulogies are given at the end of the 30-day mourning period.

Eulogies are not offered on certain days—even when funerals may be permitted in some cases. These dates include: the Sabbath, festivals, Rosh Chodesh (new moon), Hanukkah, Purim, and on the eve of a holiday and the day following it, during the entire month of Nisan, and on the days when the *tachanun* prayer (of supplication) is omitted from the daily liturgy. However, most non-Orthodox contemporary rabbis will offer a eulogy on any day in which a funeral is permitted, and many Orthodox rabbis will give eulogy on the majority of these days as well.

The eulogy should be offered in the presence of the bier, either in a public gathering place or at the cemetery. Since the funeral for scholars and community leaders took place in the synagogue (as is still the case in many communities today), rabbis offered eulogies inside the synagogue.

REFERENCES

Diament, Anita. *Saying Kaddish: How to Comfort the Dying, Bury the Dead, and Mourn as a Jew*. New York: Schocken Books, 1998.

Kay, Alan A. *A Jewish Book of Comfort*. Northvale, NJ: Jason Aronson, 1996.

Lamm, Maurice. *The Jewish Way in Death and Mourning*. Middle Village, NY: Jonathan David Publishers, 1969.

K

KABBALAT SHABBAT. This phrase literally means the reception of the Sabbath and generally refers to the welcoming of the Sabbath on Friday evening. Thus, it includes all the preparation that takes place before the Sabbath. Some people studied the weekly Torah reading prior to the Sabbath: twice in Hebrew and once in its Aramaic translation. Liturgically, *kabbalat Shabbat* refers to a section of liturgy that precedes the Friday evening worship service. While this liturgy takes place in traditional synagogues not later than one half hour after sunset, those synagogues with late night services recite this section of the liturgy just prior to the recitation of the evening service.

Influenced by the mystics in Safed, Ashkenazi Jews (whose families originally hailed from Germany) and some others added six psalms to Psalms 92 and 93 to begin the *kabbalat Shabbat* liturgy (service that introduces the Sabbath): Psalms 95–99 and 29, which correspond to the six days of creation and the six weekdays. These psalms are not shadowed by any measure of sorrow or sadness. Instead, they are exuberant in spirit.

Beginning in the sixteenth century, liturgists added several prayer poems to the service. *Lekha Dodi*, one of the most famous, fits in the middle of the recitation of these psalms (after Psalms 92–93 and before Psalms 95–99, 29). Rabbi Solomon Halevi Alkabetz, one of the circle of Kabbalists in Safed led by Rabbi Isaac Luria, wrote this song in 1540. It is now included in almost every Jewish community in the world that is influenced by the Ashkenazi rite. It follows the pattern of intricate literary devices that were in vogue at the time. The first letters of each verse spell out the author's name in an acrostic style.

Alkabetz also included numerous quotations and paraphrases from the Bible. He was influenced by a story in the Talmud (Shabbat 119a) that rehearses Rabbi Hanina and Rabbi Yannai's procedures for preparing for the Sabbath. Hanina put on his Sabbath clothes and stood at sunset and exclaimed, "Come let us welcome the Sabbath bride." Rabbi Yannai dressed in his festive clothing and called out, "Come, O bride! Come, O bride." This idea also formed the basis of the Kabbalistic custom in Safed to go out into the fields at sunset on Friday where they recited prayers and sang hymns in honor of the Sabbath. Eventually, Sabbath observers joined this practice to the liturgy in the form of *kabbalat Shabbat*. In remembrance of the early mystical practice, congregants turn toward the entrance of the synagogue and bow slightly as they sing the last stanza of *Lekha Dodi* and greet the Sabbath bride, beckoning her to join them in their midst. A growing number of Reform congregations follow this practice, but early Reformers rejected it while also shortening the liturgy of *kabblat Shabbat*.

It is customary for those who go to the synagogue for the first time in mourning to wait until the congregation finishes singing *Lekha Dodi* before entering. They wait in an anteroom or foyer. When they enter, they are greeted with "May God [using the word *Hamakom*, the Everywhere Present God] comfort you among the mourners for Zion and Jerusalem." Prior to the introduction of *kabbalat Shabbat* into the liturgy, people greeted mourners when they entered the synagogue.

Following *Lekha Dodi*, worshipers recite Psalms 95–99 and 29. Some communities recite the Song of Songs in honor of the Sabbath bride prior to the evening service. Likewise, some communities recite the hymn *Ana Bakoach* before *Lekha Dodi* (or Psalm 121).

Other communities evolved a variety of rituals to welcome the Sabbath. Some rites recite the second chapter of Mishnah Shabbat prior to the evening service. Other rites recite this chapter of Mishnah following the evening prayer service. Yemenite Jews insert liturgical poems (*piyyutim*) before the evening service on the Sabbaths that coincide with Rosh Chodesh, as well as for those Sabbaths that occur during **sefirat haomer**.

REFERENCES

Greenberg, Irving. *Guide to Shabbat*. New York: CLAL, National Jewish Center for Learning and Leadership, 1981.
Hammer, Reuven. *Entering Jewish Prayer*. New York: Schocken Books, 1994.
Heschel, Abraham Joshua. *The Sabbath: Its Meaning for Modern Man*. New York; Farrar, Straus and Giroux, 1951.
Kaplan, Aryeh. *Sabbath: Day of Eternity*. New York: National Conference of Synagogue Youth/Union of Orthodox Jewish Congregations of America, 1982.
Millgram, Abraham Ezra. *Sabbath: Day of Delight*. Philadelphia: The Jewish Publication Society of America, 1944.
Schauss, Hayyim. *A Guide to Jewish Holy Days: History and Observance*. New York: Schocken Books, 1969.
Shapiro, Mark Dov. *Gates of Shabbat*. New York: Central Conference of American Rabbis, 1991.

KAPPARAH (SHLUGGEN KAPPAROS). This custom of symbolically transferring one's sins (usually) to a fowl is practiced by some Orthodox Jews on the day before the Day of Atonement. It is virtually nonexistent among Reform and Conservative Jews. However, it does take place in some Jewish Renewal congregations in one form or another. Among some Orthodox communities, this ritual also takes place on the day before Rosh Hashanah and Hoshanah Rabbah (literally, the "Great Saving," a special day that marks the end of the Sukkot holiday before Shemini Atzeret and Simchat Torah). As part of the ceremony, the individual takes the fowl in the left hand with the right hand on the bird's head, reads Psalms 107:10, 14, 17–21 and Job 33:23–24, then swings a rooster (for a male) or a hen (for a female) around the person's head three times while saying the following: "This is my substitute, my vicarious offering, my atonement. This cock [or hen] shall meet death, but I shall find a long and pleasant life of peace." Often a parent will follow the same procedure by swinging the bird around the child's head.

In the past, immediately following the ritual, the fowl was slaughtered according to the laws of ritual slaughtering. To show compassion for God's creatures, the liver, kidneys, and other internal organs were placed outside for the birds. In some communities, it became customary to give the meat to the poor. Some communities kept the meat and made an equivalent monetary contribution to the poor.

While other animals are used among contemporary Orthodox Jews, many modern congregations use money instead.

While the ceremony considerably predates the ninth century, perhaps as a folk adaptation of the biblical scapegoat ceremony, the ritual is first discussed in the writings of the *geonim* (academy heads) of that period. Apparently, following the destruction of the second Temple in 70 C.E., people stopped using animals common to the sacrificial cult for this ritual. Some authorities (like Solomon ben Abraham Adret) objected to the rite entirely, because it approximated a sacrificial rite too closely. Likewise, he argued that the *kapparah* rite should not be practiced because it bore great similarity to heathen rituals. Conversely, Kabbalists like Isaac Luria and Isaiah Horowitz encouraged the practice by infusing it with mystical interpretations. Similarly, Moses Isserles, the editor of the Ashkenazic glosses (called the *Mapah*) on the *Shulchan Arukh* (the definitive Jewish law code) made it a compulsory rite—in response to the desire of the masses—and added the requirements of laying on of the hands, immediate slaughter of the animal, and prayers of confession.

REFERENCE

Lauterbach, Jacob Z. "The Ritual of the *Kaparot* Ceremony." In *Studies in Jewish Law, Custom, and Folklore*. New York: KTAV Publishing Co., 1970.

KERIAH. The tearing of one's garments upon hearing of the death of a member of the immediate family (defined by Jewish law as father, mother, children over 30 days old, brother, sister, husband, wife). Based on Genesis 37:34 and Job 1:20, modern Jews formalized the act of *keriah* into the ritual tearing of one's garment (or the tearing of a black ribbon affixed to one's garment) just prior to a funeral or interment. Just prior to tearing the garment (or ribbon), the individual mourner announces, "Praised are You, righteous Judge." Some argue that the requirement to tear one's clothing was moved from the moment of death to the funeral in order to prevent people from leaving the bedside of a dying family member to tear their clothing.

The rent is supposed to be four inches long, on the lapel of an outer garment. When mourning parents, the individual mourner makes the *keriah* in all clothing except for undergarments. While the *keriah* is cut on the left side of one's garments for one's parents, all other mourners make the *keriah* on the right side. The *keriah* should be exposed during the entire mourning period. However, it may be roughly stitched up following **shiva** and then completely sewn following **sheloshim** (the initial 30 days of mourning). For parents, it may be stitched up only after *sheloshim*, but it may never be completely sewn up. While Orthodox Jews still perform *keriah* in their clothing, some do so only on a tie. Most Conservative, Reconstructionist, and Reform Jews use *keriah* ribbons.

The *keriah* is delayed during *hol hamoed* (the intermediate days of festival, specifically Sukkot and Pesach) and done after the festival. An entire congregation "cuts *keriah*" if it witnessed the destruction of a Torah scroll by fire. One performs *keriah* upon seeing the Temple mount and Jerusalem in ruins. During the talmudic period, people performed *keriah* following the death of the *nasi* (president of the Sanhedrin) as well as any great scholar.

REFERENCES

Donin, Hayyim Halevy. *To Be a Jew: A Guide to Jewish Observance in Contemporary Life*. New York: Basic Books, 1991.
Hauptman, Judith. "Death and Mourning: A Time for Weeping, A Time for Healing." In *Celebration and Renewal*, edited by Rela M. Geffen. Philadelphia: The Jewish Publication Society of America, 1993, pp. 226–251.

KERIAT HATORAH. As a result of the interpretion of Exodus 15:22 as a metaphor for Torah ("they traveled three days in the wilderness and found no water"), the rabbis required that no more than three days may pass without the public reading of the Torah, *keriat haTorah*. This public reading in itself is supposed to be a reenactment or simulation of the experience of revelation. Thus, it is publicly read on Mondays and Thursdays (as designated market days) and the Sabbath. In addition, Torah is read on holidays. Some scholars suggest that the reading of the Torah was designed as an introduction to an explanatory homily.

On the Sabbath, the ritual begins with a preliminary prayer that praises God as incomparable. It also asks God to deal kindly with Zion. This prayer is eliminated on weekdays. Two prayers are said at the opening of the ark in which the Torah is housed. The first is composed of verses from the Bible (Numbers 10:35 and Isaiah 2:3).

When the Israelites broke camp and the Levites carried the ark forward, they used the words of the first verse to express their faith in God as their leader in the desert who will help them do battle with their enemies. The second verse is Isaiah's vision that Torah (which he reads as moral instruction) will go forth from Zion to the entire world. These two verses are followed by praise to God for giving the Torah to Israel. The second prayer said at the opening of the ark is taken from the *Zohar*, the primary Jewish mystical text of Jewish mystics. Many prayer books eliminate this on weekdays. Some congregations never say it.

The Torah is removed. The ark is closed. The reader and those standing with the reader face the congregation. On the Sabbath, the reader recites the first verse of the *shema* and a second line that affirms God as one and great. This is repeated by the congregation. In Reform synagogues, this is recited in unison. On weekdays, the reader begins with a different verse (*gadlu Adonai*) while facing the ark. It is the custom of many to bow slightly while reciting this text. Some also raise the Torah near the conclusion of the verse. Then the worshipers respond with *lekha Adonai* while the reader carries the Torah to the reading table. The Torah is held straight up, across the right hip, leaning slightly on the shoulder. This circuit (*hakafa* in Hebrew) is often determined by the placement of the reading table and the size of the congregation. In some Reform congregations, there are no **hakafot**, except on Simchat Torah.

In addition to the Torah reader (*baal keriah*), there are two individuals at the reading table. One serves as the *s'gan* (lieutenant or assistant to the reader) and the other as the *gabbai* (manager). (Some refer to these individuals as *gabbai* and *gabbai sheni*.) Both follow the reading of the text and correct the mistakes of the reader according to specific guidelines established for this purpose. While there are traditional duties assigned to each, in many congregations these roles have been conflated. In some congregations, only one *gabbai* is used. And in some congregations, there is no *gabbai*.

After the Torah is placed on the reading table and prepared for reading, the reader or *gabbai* recites an introductory prayer. (Different versions are used for weekdays and the Sabbath.) For the public reading to be fully understood by the listener, someone must translate it into the vernacular language. While most modern synagogues provide worshipers with the translation in printed form, in the ancient synagogue a *meturgeman* (translator) translated the Torah following its reading. This translation is called the *targum* (literally "translation"). As the Jewish people moved into other lands, scholars translated the Torah into other languages and read these translations in the synagogue following the reading of the Torah. However, during the introduction of the Greek translation into Alexandria, the Hebrew reading fell into disuse.

Following the practices for an **aliyah**, individuals are called to recite a blessing before the Torah reading. Originally, one individual read the entire reading. Later, the reading was divided into sections read by different individuals. The number increased according to the sanctity of the day. Finally, those called forward simply recited a blessing. Another individual actually read from the text. Originally, only one blessing preceded and succeeded the entire reading, rather than a blessing prior to and following each section of the Torah reading as is currently the practice. Prior to the reading of the *maftir* (additional) portion, a half-kaddish is recited. Following the reading of the final section, individuals are called forward for the honor of **hagbah** and **gelilah**. The individual doing *hagbah* raises the Torah and then shows the text to the congregation. Maimonidies suggests that the person doing *hagbah* unrolls the Torah so that the congregation can see three columns of the text, as well as one seam between sections of parchment. People chant a verse (beginning with *zot haTorah*, "this is the Torah"). Afterwards, the person honored with *hagbah* sits on a chair so that the Torah may be wrapped and covered by the person honored with *gelilah*. The raising was originally included at the start of the Torah reading during a time of great sectarianism so people could be sure that the correct text was being read. It later found its way to the end of the Torah reading. However, Sephardic synagogues still raise the Torah before it is read. In some synagogues, as the Torah is lifted and *zot haTorah* is chanted, congregants point to the Torah with the little finger of the right hand, often wrapped in a **tzitzit**.

While there is a minimum requirement of three verses per *aliyah*, there are some exceptions on holidays where the reading was not lengthened to accommodate this requirement. This is probably why the rabbis added readings for special Sabbaths.

The **haftarah** (a selection from the Prophets) is only read on the Sabbath and holidays and only after the Torah has been dressed. The Torah is usually held by a seated individual or placed in a specially designed stand while someone else is reading the ***haftarah***. In some congregations, while the Torah is being dressed, a series of prayers is read, asking for the welfare of its congregants.

After the Torah has been rolled together and covered, the reader takes it in his right hand, faces the worshipers, and begins the recitation of a series of verses from Psalm 148: 13–14. The Torah is carried in a procession once again, in the opposite direction from the earlier procession. On the Sabbath the congregation chants Psalm 29, and on weekdays the congregation chants Psalm 24. Following the procession, the reader recites Numbers 10:36, the verse Moses spoke when the ark came to rest in the wilderness. Finally, just before the ark is closed, the congregation chants Lamentations 5:21. It is a plea from a penitent people that it may be renewed and restored to its former glory.

There are two basic systems for the weekly reading of the Torah. The Torah is divided into 54 portions that are assigned to weeks throughout the year. The distribution of these portions changes from year to year depending on the holiday calendar. Thus, on occasion, several shorter portions are "doubled," that is, they are joined with the portion that either precedes or succeeds it. The practice of the Babylonian rabbis was to read the entire portion each week and conclude the entire Torah after one year. The practice of the rabbis in the land of Israel (the Palestinian tradition, as it is called) was to only read a third of the portion each week. Thus, the entire Torah is completed every three years.

As part of the liberal approach to reading the Torah in Reform congregations, a variety of practices emerged. First, some members of the Reform movement eliminated all or part of readings that were deemed inappropriate or distasteful. This practice has virtually been eliminated except for some of the selections for the holidays. It remains common to read a selection of the portion that might be relevant to what the rabbi would be explaining or expanding on in the sermon. In addition, the reader (often the rabbi) in the Reform congregation may read the entire selection. In all cases, the completion of the reading of the entire Torah over the period of a year is celebrated annually on Simchat Torah.

REFERENCES

Elbogen, Ismar. *Jewish Liturgy: A Comprehensive History*. Philadelphia and New York: The Jewish Publication Society and The Jewish Theological Seminary of America, 1993.

Mann, Jacob. *The Bible as Read and Preached in the Ancient Synagogue*. Cincinnati: Hebrew Union College Press, 1940.

KERIAT SHEMA AL HAMETAH. The custom of reciting the *shema* on retiring for the night evolved from the idea that humans need to reflect on Divine protection before entering the vulnerable state of sleep. While it may have been practiced earlier, its requirement can be traced to the time of the Mishnah (ca. 200 C.E.). It was included in the majority of prayer books. However, once the *maariv* (evening worship) service (also called *arvit*, "night time") was recited early in the evening, this became the last prayer of the day. The name refers to the central part of the prayer, which is the first paragraph of the *shema* prayer. In addition, one recites the *ha-mappil* prayer to God, "Who causes the bands of sleep to fall upon my eyes" (Babylonian Talmud, Berakhot 60b). Some authorities argue that *ha-mappil* should be recited first so that the *shema* is last on one's lips before slumber. Some even suggest its repetition until sleep overtakes the individual. As sleep imitates death, this ritual is related to the requirement that the individual recite the *shema* prior to death.

This night prayer is prophylactic. This idea is derived from Psalm 4:51: "Tremble and do not sin. Commune with your heart upon your bed and be still." Some scholars suggested, therefore, that if one spent the night studying, the *shema* was unnecessary or a simple text like Psalm 31:6 ("I commend my spirit into Your hand") was enough. (See Babylonian Talmud, Berakhot 5a–b.) Grooms were exempt from this requirement for a time. Authorities felt that the anxiety of the evening would prevent them from mustering the requisite concentration for prayer. However, later authorities argued that most people generally lacked the appropriate concentration. As is the case with most of Jewish liturgy, additional prayers have been added over time. These include Psalms 91, 3 and certain sections of the evening worship service. Kabbalistic influence can also be seen in the addition of angelology texts such as Genesis 48:16. Individuals are exempt from these additional texts on the first night of Passover, because Passover itself is a "night of watching for God" (Exodus 12: 42).

REFERENCES

Elbogen, Ismar. *Jewish Liturgy: A Comprehensive History*, translated by Raymond P. Scheindlin. Philadelphia: Jewish Publication Society, 1993.
Hammer, Reuven. *Entering Jewish Prayer*. New York: Schocken Books, 1979.
Klein, Isaac. *A Guide to Jewish Religious Practice*. New York: The Jewish Theological Seminary of America, 1979.
Millgram, Abraham. *Jewish Worship*. Philadelphia: The Jewish Publication Society of America, 1971.

KETUBAH. The *ketubah* (marriage certificate) is a wedding contract, a legal document that must be written, as provided by Jewish law, with two witnesses who are not related to groom or bride. Contemporary *ketubot* (plural) make provisions for both the bride and groom to sign the document, although this is not necessary according to traditional Jewish law. It is necessary to make a symbolic agreement (*kinyan*) with the groom. This is often done by the rabbi giving him a handkerchief to hold or some other article of clothing. The groom agrees to the obligations as stipulated in the *ketubah*. The *ketubah* is signed before the ceremony. Customarily, it is read aloud during the ceremony. Afterwards, it is given by the groom to the bride and it is considered her personal possession. However, some Reform rabbis are now including the *ketubah* signing in the midst of the ceremony itself. In addition, some Reform rabbis do not require a *ketubah*. Instead, a certificate of marriage is signed by the rabbi and two witnesses and presented to the couple but not read during the ceremony.

Often in egalitarian settings, a nontraditional *ketubah* is used, which includes both bride and groom and is more symbolic than legal. Conservative rabbis often use a *ketubah* that contains an additional clause stating that should the marriage ever be dissolved under civil law, either party may approach a Conservative rabbinical court in order to determine "what action by either spouse is then appropriate under Jewish matrimonial law; and if either spouse shall fail to honor the demand of the other or to carry out the decision of the *bet din* (rabbinical court) or its representatives, then the other spouse may invoke any and all remedies available in civil law and equity to enforce compliance with the *bet din*'s decision and this solemn obligation." This amendment was introduced to protect the woman against the possibility of a husband who might refuse to give his wife a Jewish religious divorce, which would then prevent her from remarrying in a religious ceremony.

While there is no mention of the *ketubah* in the Bible, wedding documents can be traced back to approximately 440 B.C.E. Some scholars trace the idea to the Babylonian exile. In the ancient world, marriage was a business transaction. Women were treated as a form of property. Thus, the earliest marriage documents were similar to commercial agreements. However, the form of the document changed into a listing of legal rights for the bride following the formalization of the marriage contract by the Sanhedrin in the first century B.C.E. As Jewish law was flexible in allowing for the husband to divorce his wife, the rabbis felt it necessary to protect the legal rights of the wife. A return of the dowry and other property was written directly into the document. This also served to discourage men from simply discarding their wives. Jewish law certainly permitted men more control in divorce. However, the *ketubah* elevated the rights of women in the ancient world. Fixed monetary terms were included. While today these amounts are largely symbolic, the *ketubah* still indicates a specified amount of money as the dowry. In addition, the *ketubah* stipulates that the bride will receive a specific amount of money from her husband should the marriage end in divorce.

The *ketubah* is written in Aramaic, the language of the Jews of the Second Commonwealth, the time period that indicates the second time in which the Jewish people was self-governing. In addition to the monetary terms, the husband agrees to "work for you, honor and support and maintain you according to the customs of Jewish husbands who work for their wives and who honor, support, and maintain them truthfully." New *ketubot* are often written in Aramaic and English and include parallel declarations of bride and groom followed by a joint declaration of commitment to God, Torah, and Israel.

REFERENCES

Diament, Anita. *The New Jewish Wedding*. New York: Summit Books, 1985.
Goodman, Philip and Hanna. *The Jewish Marriage Anthology*. Philadelphia: The Jewish Publication Society of America, 1965.
Routtenberg, Lilly S., and Ruth R. Seldin. *The Jewish Wedding Book*. New York: Schocken Books, 1967.

KIDDUSH. Literally "sanctification," *kiddush* is derived from the term "to sanctify." When the word *kiddush* is used alone, it generally refers to the prayer recited over a cup of wine at home or in the synagogue to consecrate the Sabbath or festival in fulfillment of the biblical command to "remember the Sabbath day and keep it holy" (Exodus 20:8; Babylonian Talmud, Pesachim 106a). While *kiddush* is considered to be a time-bound commandment from which women are generally exempt, it is one of the few such requirements that women are traditionally obligated to observe. The primary *kiddush* is said on the eve of the Sabbath or festival before the meal, as one is forbidden from eating on these occasions before reciting *kiddush*.

The ritual begins with an introductory paragraph from Genesis 1: 31 and 2:1–3 (omitted on festivals). The line "the sixth day, the heavens and earth were created" is emphasized because its words form an acronym for the four-letter name of God, the tetragrammaton. The second half of the blessing focuses on creation and the exodus from Egypt. This is the paradigm for all physical and spiritual redemption and rebirth and concludes with the sanctification of the Sabbath. The actual blessing over the wine is recited, followed by the blessing for the sanctification of the day. Before authorities made the sequencing of this ritual definite, the schools of Shammai and Hillel differed regarding whether the blessing over the wine should precede the blessing for the day or the blessing for the day should take precedence. On all full festivals (except for the last days of Pesach), the *Shehechayanu* prayer is added at the end of the ritual. When a festival immediately follows the Sabbath, a special form of **havdalah** is added.

While it is traditional to say *kiddush* over wine, many use grape juice today as a result of a growing awareness of Jews in recovery from chemical addiction. Authorities in prior generations permitted grape juice as an alternative to wine, particularly for children. It is also permissible to use two loaves of bread instead of wine when wine is not obtainable.

Kiddush is to be said at home. However, often synagogues recited it at the end of evening services. Despite the opposition of some rabbis, many congregations encouraged the recitation of *kiddush* in the synagogue for the benefit of travelers whom they fed and housed in rooms adjoining the synagogue. Except in Israel, Ashkenazim continue routinely to recite *kiddush* in the synagogue.

A minor *kiddush* (that includes a blessing over the wine but not over the day) is said on the morning of the Sabbath or festival prior to lunch, which is considered the first meal of the day or the second meal of the Sabbath/festival.

The ritual of *kiddush*, which follows the lighting of candles and precedes the saying of **hamotzi** (the prayer over bread) begins with some biblical verses that are followed by the blessing over wine. In addition to two loaves of bread, strong drink or anything that may be considered the national beverage of the land may be used instead of wine.

In the modern synagogue, *kiddush* also refers to the social hour following Sabbath (often called Oneg Shabbat) and festival services.

REFERENCES

Donin, Hayyim Halevy. *To Be a Jew: A Guide to Contemporary Observance.* New York: Basic Books, 1991.

Elbogen, Ismar. *Jewish Liturgy: A Comprehensive History*, translated by Raymond P. Scheindlin. Philadelphia: Jewish Publication Society, 1993.

Klein, Isaac. *A Guide to Jewish Religious Practice.* New York: The Jewish Theological Seminary of America, 1979.

Wolfson, Ron. *The Shabbat Seder.* Woodstock, VT: Jewish Lights Publishing, 1996.

KIDDUSH HACHAMAH. The blessing of the sun that is held only once every 28 years, the *kiddush hachamah* is a short prayer service in which individuals bless the sun and thank God for creating it and placing it into motion on the fourth day of creation (see Genesis 1: 16–19). The ritual ceremony takes place following morning services when the sun is about 90° above the eastern horizon, on the first Wednesday of the month of Nisan, when the vernal equinox (*makhzor gadol*) begins, according to Rabbi Abbaye (see Babylonian Talmud, Berakhot 59b). Although Abbaye's method for determining the specific day for this ritual became obsolete when the Jewish community adopted Rabbi Adda's system of calendation, the ceremony did not fall into disuse.

The ritual begins with the recitation of these biblical verses: Psalms 84:12, 72:5, 75:2; Malachi 3:20; Psalms 97:6 and 148. This is followed by a benediction that praises God as the Maker of Creation. Next come Psalms 19 and 121, which are followed by the singing of the hymn *El Adon* (from the Shabbat morning liturgy). The ritual continues with the reciting of the *baraita* (rabbinic teaching) of Abbaye (Babylonian Talmud, Berakhot 59b), which enjoins the community to engage in the ritual and then is followed by a series of quotations of an *aggadah* (rabbinic story that elucidates the Torah) by R. Hananiah ben Akashya in the Mishnah (Makkot 3:16). The ritual concludes with a short prayer of thanksgiving in which members of the community thank God for allowing them to live to see this day and optimistically ask that they may live to reach the days of the Messiah and the fulfillment of the prophecy of Isaiah "and the light if the sun shall be sevenfold as the light of the seven days" (Isaiah 30:26).

REFERENCES

Donin, Hayyim Halevy. *To Be a Jew: A Guide to Contemporary Observance.* New York: Basic Books, 1991.

Elbogen, Ismar. *Jewish Liturgy: A Comprehensive History*, translated by Raymond P. Scheindlin. Philadelphia: Jewish Publication Society, 1993.

Klein, Isaac. *A Guide to Jewish Religious Practice.* New York: The Jewish Theological Seminary of America, 1979.

KIDDUSH LEVANAH. According to the Talmud, any person who witnesses an important natural event is required to say a blessing (Babylonian Talmud, Berakhot 54a); thus, the appearance of the new moon gives rise to the expression of an individual in praise of the Creator in the ritual of *kiddush levanah*, or sanctification of the moon. But the ritual probably also provides the Jewish people with a symbol of its capacity to regenerate itself in much the same way as the moon seems to do each month. Psalm 89:38 draws out the relationship between the moon and the Davidic dynasty. This ritual of *kiddush levanah*, which includes *birkat levanah* (blessing of the moon) as its focal point, is recited when the moon is clearly visible in the sky. The words for the blessing can be found in the Talmud (Sanhedrin 42a).

The ritual usually takes place between the seventh and fifteenth day of the Hebrew month. However, it may take place as early as the third, and some Hasidim wait until the tenth day. The ritual should not take place during the second half of the month, which is considered to be past the fourteenth or fifteenth of the month. However, it is customary in Israel to say it immediately after the appearance of the moon. The ritual must take place while individuals are standing, facing east, at night following the evening worship service, out in the open or at a window or near an open door. Saturday night is preferable (if it occurs before the tenth of the month), because people are still dressed for Shabbat. The evening following a holiday is also preferred for the same reason. However, one should not say *kiddush levanah* before Tisha B'av or Yom Kippur because of their solemn character. It may be said following Yom Kippur and is often said just after the conclusion of Yom Kippur services. Others say it before Yom Kippur. Those who say it following Tisha B'av should remember to put on leather shoes that had been taken off for its observance. Mourners are generally exempt from the ritual unless there is no other time for them to say it.

In recent years, the nascent Jewish men's movement has taken on *kiddush levanah* as its standard, probably in reaction to the women's claim on Rosh Chodesh or because traditionally women are exempt from this ritual. Some authorities suggest that women are actually prohibited from performing the ritual.

REFERENCES

Donin, Hayyim Halevy. *To Be a Jew: A Guide to Contemporary Observance.* New York: Basic Books, 1991.
Elbogen, Ismar. *Jewish Liturgy: A Comprehensive History,* translated by Raymond P. Scheindlin. Philadelphia: Jewish Publication Society, 1993.
Klein, Isaac. *A Guide to Jewish Religious Practice.* New York: The Jewish Theological Seminary of America, 1979.
Lipschutz, Chaim U. *Kiddush Levono, The Monthly Blessing of the Moon.* Brooklyn, NY: Maznaim Publishers, 1987.

KIDDUSHIN. Alternatively called *erusin, kiddushin* is the wedding ceremony. The term previously referred to only the ritual of betrothal, which is now part of the wedding ceremony. There is very little material in the Bible that actually describes a wedding ceremony. As the act of marriage is described simply as "taking"—as in "when a man takes a wife" (Deuteronomy 24:1)—one must draw conclusions based on statements that are related to weddings. In the story of Jacob's marriage, however, it is clear that some sort of celebration took place. There the Torah states, "Laban gathered all the people of the place and made a feast" (Genesis 29:22). A the same time, the text refers to a bridal week. When Jacob learns of Laban's deception and wants to marry Rachel immediately, he is told, "Wait until the bridal week of this one is over and we will give you this one too" (Genesis 29:27).

There are other descriptions, as well. Processions with musical accompaniment of the bride and groom were central to the celebrations. There are also many references to bridal attire and adornment.

It also seems that the community included the exhibition of a blood-stained sheet (evidence of the bride's virginity) in the ceremony.

During the talmudic period (and presumably before the Common Era), the marriage ceremony was divided into two parts. The first is called *kiddushin* (separation, consecration) or *erusin* (betrothal). This was effected by the groom handing over something of value to the bride in the presence of witnesses and reciting the formula, "Behold, you are consecrated to me with this ring according to the law of Moses and Israel." The ring actually is a modern substitute for something of value that the groom used to purchase his bride from her father. Two blessings were recited, one over wine and one over the actual act of betrothal. Some suggest that the second blessing contained a warning to the bride and groom not to cohabit until the actual marriage ceremony, called *nissuin*, that took place at a later time (usually a year later in the case of a virgin, one who was neither divorced nor widowed). While many liberal couples exchange rings, legal authorities argue against it, because it undermines the *kinyan* (acquisition) aspect of the ceremony. Some brides therefore give their grooms the ring separately as a gift, often during **yichud**.

The second part of the ceremony was also called **chuppah** (canopy) after the groom's house to which the bride was led. Originally *nissuin* was effected simply by the bride entering the groom's house and cohabitating with him. On the occasion of the *nissuin*, additional blessings were recited. After this stage the couple was fully married. Technically, according to traditional Jewish law, once the bride enters the *chuppah*, she becomes married. Thus, the legal phrase "acquired" is used. While the term *chuppah* originally took on a variety of meanings, it now refers solely to the wedding canopy itself.

During the post-talmudic period, probably beginning in the Middle Ages, authorities joined these two separate rituals into one ceremony that took place at one time. Some theorize that this was a result of the perilous conditions in which the Jews lived. A few *adot hamizrach* (eastern) communities did not combine the two ceremonies. Modern rabbis added a variety of elements to the wedding ceremony, including several prayers, a sermon or wedding charge, and a blessing over the bridal couple.

There is no regulation as to where a wedding can be held. Many choose the synagogue. And among many, the ceremony takes place outside in the open. This custom probably reflects the ideal of evening ceremony so that the stars can be seen, reminding the community of God's promise to Abraham that his descendants would be as numerous as the stars in the heaven (see Genesis 22:17). Tuesday is a popular day for weddings among Orthodox Jews, because in the story of creation, the Torah reminds us that following the third day, "God saw that this was good" (Genesis 1:10, 12). A wedding may take place any day except for the Sabbath, festivals, three weeks before the 17th of Tammuz and the 9th of Av, as well as the *sefirah* period, which marks the time between Pesach and Shavuot excluding Lag B'Omer. Some Reform rabbis officiate during the restricted period of the three weeks, during the period of the Omer, and on Tisha B'av. A minority of Reform rabbis permit weddings to take place on Shabbat. Among Sephardim, weddings do not take place on Lag B'Omer, but are permitted on the day after and during the remainder of the Omer period.

No specific dress is required for a wedding. In the Orthodox community, the groom usually wears a *kittel* (burial shroud). This is probably a result of the comparison of the wedding to the Day of Atonement when the *kittel* is worn. Sometimes the groom wears a **tallit**, as does the officiating rabbi on occasion. Depending on their communities of origin, some brides and grooms wear elaborate costumes.

In anticipation of the wedding ceremony (although technically part of it), the groom undertakes the obligation of the **ketubah** (wedding contract) through the act of *kinyan* (acquisition). This ritual is executed by the rabbi taking a piece of cloth from the groom, which he then returns to the groom. Witnesses sign the document (in some places, such as Israel, so does the groom). The groom is then escorted to where the bride is waiting and lets down her veil (this is part of the **bedeken** ritual). Here the officiant pronounces over the bride, "O sister! May you grow into thousands of myriads," a text taken from Genesis 24:60. This is not common among Reform Jews.

Next the groom is led to the wedding canopy by both fathers (or other male relatives, if the bride or groom is fatherless). Once he arrives at the wedding canopy, he stands facing the land of Israel. The bride is led to the wedding canopy by both mothers. The couple is invited forward to the *chuppah* by a formulaic chant. Among Ashkenazim, the bride walks around the groom seven times (three times in some communities), then stands to the right of the groom. Next the rabbi offers a wedding charge or short sermon. This is followed by the wine and marriage blessing (the remnant of the independent betrothal ceremony). The father gives the bridegroom the wine to drink, while the mother gives the bride wine to drink. In many communities, the cup of wine is given to the couple by the rabbinic officiant. In some communities, the cup of wine is shared with members of the immediate family and sometimes with close friends. The rabbi may even offer the wine to grandparents, who are seated close to the *chuppah*. The bride may hold the cup for her future in-laws, while the groom would do the same for his.

In order for all to see, the groom then places the wedding ring on the forefinger of the bride's right hand as he recites the traditional formula of consecration. Some suggest that this finger is used because it was believed that it was connected to an artery that went directly to the heart. Others say that rings were once worn on that finger (a practice that has gained recent popularity once again). By placing the ring on the bride's most active finger, she is acknowledging that this is a binding legal transaction and not merely a gift. This aspect of the ceremony is the central act of *kiddushin*. In some communities, the groom breaks a glass under his foot at this time in the ceremony (see **breaking of the glass**). The *ketubah* is read aloud by the rabbi or another individual whom the couple chooses to honor. This divides the ceremony into two parts and separates the betrothal from the actual wedding.

Seven blessings (***sheva berakhot***) are chanted. While only two legal witnesses are needed for the wedding, a *minyan* is required for the recital of the seven blessings. The father now gives the bride wine to drink and the mother gives the groom wine to drink. In some Sephardic communities, parents sometimes cover bride and groom with a *tallit* during the seven blessings. The groom crushes a separate glass under his foot. (In some communities the glass is thrown against the wall.) The couple is then escorted to a private room for the symbolic ritual of ***yichud*** (literally "of making one," consummation). In most Reform, Conservative, and Reconstructionist ceremonies, even the symbolic nature of *yichud* is often dismissed.

Many customs surround the ritual of the marriage ceremony. Some reflect a desire to keep evil away from the bridal couple. Others are designed to invoke blessings of fertility. And still others are simple reflections of the joy felt by friends and family at the time of the wedding.

In most non-Orthodox situations where a *ketubah* is read, some of the language has been changed to reflect the egalitarian nature of the wedding and to prevent certain legal problems that have arisen in the course of history, such as the *agunah* (literally "chained") or deserted woman. In addition, there has been a great deal of discussion in the Conservative movement over the use of the term *betulta* (virgin) in the *ketubah* when referring to the bride.

REFERENCES

Diament, Anita. *The New Jewish Wedding*. New York: Simon and Schuster, 1985.
Lamm, Maurice. *The Jewish Way of Love and Marriage*. San Francisco: Harper and Row, 1980.

KIPPAH. While some men cover their heads with hats, most will use a specially designed skull cap called a *kippah* (in Hebrew) or *yarmulkeh* (in Yiddish). Some married women choose to cover their heads with hats or lace while reciting a blessing or engaged in prayer. Traditional Jewish women often cover their hair completely (with a wig or hat) as a sign of modesty. However, in the synagogue, they cover their hair with a hat whether or not they are wearing a wig. In the past, unmarried women who wore their hair loosely or exposed were considered sexually frivolous. All women were required to cover their hair during the reading of the *shema*, thus making it mandatory in the synagogue. While it was a minority position in the traditional Jewish community, as it became stylish for women to wear their hair uncovered, some authorities permitted the practice. It has become increasingly more common for more liberal women to wear *kippot* (plural of *kippah*) during study or worship.

Technically, while covering the head may be more correctly labeled a custom rather than a ritual, it is so closely associated with ritual acts that it is included here. There are a variety of opinions regarding the practice. Some authorities suggest that it emerged as a special act of the pious. Others argued that it was a mandatory act for everyone. Specifics about the history of this practice are also not clear. In some countries, the practice was unknown. In other countries, the practice was reserved for certain activities such as prayer, the study of sacred texts, and the performance of a religious ritual. In communities of the Mediterranean that were influenced by Babylonian custom during the hegemony of the Islamic empires, authorities insisted on worshipers covering their heads. Conversely, in communities influenced by the custom of the land of Israel, such as those in France, Germany, and Italy, Jews may not have initially worshiped with uncovered heads. The custom of men covering the head eventually spread and became standard in Germany and Central Europe from the thirteenth century onward. It probably resulted as an imitation of the women's custom to cover the head when the practice of men wearing a *tallit katan* (small four-cornered fringe garment, also called *arba kanfot*, literally "four corners") under clothing rather than over clothing evolved. Males sought an external way of displaying their commitment to the covenant with God. Thus, approximately for the past hundred years it has become the practice for traditionally observant Jews to keep their heads covered at all times. According to Maimonides, the act was a display of reverence and respect. In addition, since non-Jews kept their heads uncovered, the covering of the head by Jews was an identifying act that served as a bulwark against assimilation.

Immediately following the Six Day War in 1967, an increasing number of Jews who were not traditionally observant covered their head as a sign of their Jewish identity and proud alliance with the state of Israel. Historically, Reform Judaism discarded the practice, though some Reform Jews adhered to it. Today, an increasing number of Reform Jews cover their heads for prayer, study, and ritual, and there are some Reform rabbis who keep their head covered at all times. Customarily, Conservative Jews cover their heads when in the synagogue, when praying or studying sacred literature, or when eating because of the benedictions required. (Formerly, some followed the German custom of covering the head only while saying the benedictions.) While many Conservative rabbis keep their heads covered at all times, few laypersons do so.

REFERENCES

Krauss, Samuel. "The Jewish Rite of Covering the Head." *Hebrew Union College Annual* vol. 19 (1944–45), pp. 121–168.
Lauterbach, Jacob. "Worshipping with Covered Heads." In Jacob Schwartz, *Responsa of the CCAR*. New York: Union of American Hebrew Congregations, 1954, pp. 208–218; reprinted in Jacob Lauterbach, *Studies in Jewish Law, Custom and Folklore*. New York: KTAV Publishing Co., 1970, pp. 225–235.

KOL HANE'ARIM. Literally "all the children," *kol hane'arim* is the **aliyah**, or Torah honor, for children. (It is alternatively called *aliyot ne'arim* or *hatarat ne'arim*.) This is the last *aliyah* that precedes the bridegroom's *aliyot* (**chatan Torah** and **chatan bereishit**) during Simchat Torah when the concluding portion of Deuteronomy 33 is read. This is read over and over again until each adult who wants an *aliyah* is given one. Then children under the age of Bar Mitzvah (**Bar/Bat Mitzvah** in Reform, Reconstructionist, and egalitarian Conservative synagogues) are called to the honor of the Torah. In traditional congregations, infants are held by their fathers, while in egalitarian congregations, either mother or father brings the child forward to the Torah. Several large *tallitot* (plural of ***tallit***) are held aloft to cover the children as a canopy.

The actual *aliyah* blessing is said by an adult, who is joined by the voices of these children. Following the second blessing, the rabbi and the congregation bless the children with the classic blessing of Jacob over Ephraim and Manasseh (see Genesis 48:16): "The angel who redeems me from all evil will bless the children and call them in my name and the name of my ancestors Abraham and Isaac; and may they multiply and increase in the midst of the land." In those congregations where girls are also invited, the parallel blessing is used (the same one that is used for daughters on Friday evening at the Shabbat table). In some congregations, immediately following the *aliyah*, children are showered with candy while the congregation sings, "And you shall see children born to your children. Let there be peace in Israel."

REFERENCES

Chill, Abraham. *The Minhagim: The Customs and Ceremonies of Judaism, Their Origins and Rationale*. New York: Sepher-Hermon Press, 1979.

Greenberg, Irving. *The Jewish Way: Living the Holidays*. New York: Summit Books, 1988.

Isaacs, Ronald. *Every Person's Guide to Sukkot, Shemini Atzeret and Simchat Torah*. Northvale, NJ: Jason Aronson, 1999.

Strassfeld, Michael. *The Jewish Holidays: A Guide and Commentary*. New York: Harper & Row, 1985.

Waskow, Arthur I. *Seasons of Our Joy: A Handbook of Jewish Festivals*. New York: Summit Books, 1986.

L

LEVAYAH. Funeral, *lavayah* in Hebrew, is also called *levayat hamet* ("accompanying the dead"). While there is no fixed ritual for a funeral, most funerals share some common elements whether they take place in a home, synagogue, mortuary, or at the grave. Often, funerals include a service at home, synagogue or mortuary, which is followed by a brief interment service at the grave. With few exceptions, funerals (and the subsequent interment) must take place within twenty-four hours of death. Among Reform Jews, this requirement is more flexible. Traditionally, only the funerals of rabbis (or community leaders) took place in the synagogue. Thus, the Conservative movement requires that the body not be brought into the sanctuary—when possible—where the service takes place.

The format for a funeral generally includes a psalm, a scriptural passage, and the memorial prayer *El maleh rachamim*. In the immediate past, eulogies were reserved for community dignitaries. However, it is now customary to offer a eulogy prior to the memorial prayer for everyone. Funerals for community leaders often take place in the synagogue. The eulogy may be given by the officiant (rabbi) or a member of the family, following the Talmudic injunction, "Just as the dead shall be called to account, so shall the eulogizers be called to account" (Babylonian Talmud, Berakhot 62a). When the *tachanun* (supplication) prayer is not recited, then the eulogy is also to be omitted. It is also excluded when funerals take place on Friday afternoon, or on the afternoon preceding a festival. However, Reform Jews and some Conservative and Reconstructionist Jews do not to follow this practice and offer a eulogy nonetheless. In some communities, the cutting of **keriah** takes place before or after the funeral prior to the interment.

Among Sephardic Jews, children ask the deceased for forgiveness as part of what is called *mechilah*. This takes place before the **blowing of the shofar** after the **mourner's** *kaddish*. The shofar is blown only for a man with children. Then the service concludes with the recitation of Psalm 91 for a man and Proverbs 31 for a woman.

There is a difference in practice among communities regarding the order of the procession when the coffin leaves the home or mortuary. In some places, the mourners lead, followed by the coffin carried by pallbearers and then the rest of the people. In other communities, the coffin is carried out first. It is common practice today for the mourners to lead, followed by the rest of the people, and then the coffin follows. Often the matter of procession is determined by convenience rather than ritual practice. In the past, the pallbearers actually carried the coffin to the cemetery. Due to the distance of cemeteries, the pallbearers usually carry the coffin (or guide it on a rolling cart made for this purpose) to a hearse, which is then driven to the cemetery. It is customary for the hearse to stop in front of the synagogue where the deceased worshiped. It is also customary in some communities to stop several times (the specific number is debated) on the way to the cemetery. In ancient times, it was customary to stop seven times on the way to the grave. It may have simply been a custom that evolved to lessen the burden of carrying the coffin on the shoulders of pallbearers.

At the cemetery, pallbearers carry the coffin from the hearse to the grave. The graveside service usually includes *tzidduk hadin*, a prayerful acknowledgment of Divine justice in the act of death. When the *tzidduk hadin* prayer is recited, it is also traditional to stop seven times on the way to the grave while reciting Psalm 91. A variety of reasons have been suggested for the seven stops, including the seven stages of life as mentioned in Ecclesiastes Rabbah 1:1 (midrash on the book of Ecclesiastes) and the number of times the word *hevel* ("vanity") is mentioned in the book of Ecclesiastes. Others suggest that this is just a means to give mourners additional time to reflect on the meaning of the deceased's life and the vanities that may be mistaken for a meaningful life.

After the coffin has been placed in the grave, it is lowered. Following the reading of the *tzidduk hadin*, the memorial prayer *El moleh rachamim*, and then the **mourner's *kaddish***, mourners place a few spadefuls of earth on the coffin. Jewish law, however, states that the grave must be covered with earth before *kaddish* can be read. In some communities, a special *kaddish* (*kaddish itchadeta*) said only at the graveside is recited. (On days when *tachanun* prayers are not said, Psalm 16 is read in place of the *tzidduk hadin*.) Most liberal services end with the reciting of "God has given. God has taken. Praised be the name of God" (Job 1:21). In many Reform congregations, mourners do not place dirt on the grave. Following the service at the cemetery, those gathered form two lines and allow mourners to pass through them. As the mourners pass, those assembled offer condolences with the traditional formula: "May God comfort you among the mourners for Zion and Jerusalem."

Before leaving the cemetery, it is customary to wash one's hands ritually. In some communities, it is the practice to wash one's hands prior to entering the house of mourning when returning from the cemetery. It is also a widespread custom to pick a sprig of grass as one leaves the cemetery and say, "And they blossom out of the city like the grass of the earth" (Psalm 72:16) and "God remembers that we are dust" (Psalm 103:14). Both verses reflect an affirmation of the frailty of life and the hope for resurrection.

REFERENCES

Diament, Anita. *Saying Kaddish: How to Comfort the Dying, Bury the Dead, and Mourn as a Jew*. New York: Schocken Books, 1998.

Dobrinsky, Henry. *A Treasury of Sephardic Laws and Customs: The Ritual Practices of Syrian, Moroccan, Judeo-Spanish and Spanish and Portuguese Jews of North America*. Hoboken, NJ, and New York: KTAV and Yeshiva University Press, 1986.

Kay, Alan A. *A Jewish Book of Comfort*. Northvale, NJ: Jason Aronson, 1993.

Lamm, Maurice. *The Jewish Way in Death and Mourning*. Middle Village, NY: Jonathan David Publishers, 1969.

Wieseltier, Leon. *Kaddish*. New York: Alfred A. Knopf, Inc., 1998.

LULAV. Specifically referring to the shoot of the palm tree (which has remained in its folded state) used on Sukkot, *lulav* more generally refers to a combined branch of palm, myrtle, and willow, three of the four species (palm/*lulav*, myrtle/*hadasim*, willow/*aravot*, and citron/*etrog*) required for use on the Sukkot holiday. While any palm may be used, the date palm is the most common. Similarly, as the tradition is not particular about the species of willow, local willows are generally used. The *lulav* itself should measure at least three handbreadths in length. The rabbis deduce this requirement from the instruction of Leviticus 23:40: "On the first day you shall take the product of *hadar* trees [interpreted as the citron], branches of palm trees, boughs of leafy trees [interpreted as myrtle] and willows of the brook." The three species are bound together by palm leaves. Today a woven basket-like structure from palm leaves is commonly used. The *lulav* should have one palm branch, two willow branches, and three myrtle twigs. They should be tied together in the direction in which they grow, with the myrtle on the right and the willow on the left of the palm branch, by three rings made of palm leaves to represent the patriarchs. The spine of the palm branch should face the person holding the *lulav*. Taken with the *etrog*, the *lulav* is waved during morning services according to the following specific formula that evolved from the description of the festival in Leviticus 23:40.

Before Hallel (Psalms 113–118), individuals recite the benediction over both the *lulav* and the *etrog*. They are held during the entire time Hallel is recited. While technically one can perform the ritual of waving the *lulav* anytime during the day (but not at night), it is preferably done in the morning with the *lulav* just before and during Hallel. The *lulav* is taken in the right hand with the *etrog* in the left hand, held together in the position in which the *etrog* grows. The *etrog* is reversed during the benediction and then reversed once again and held together with the *lulav* in preparation for the waving. Together, touching, they are waved in six directions in this sequence: east, south, west, north, up, down. Each wave includes a forward and backward motion and is accompanied by the shaking of the leaves of the *lulav*. The waving also takes place each time the word *hodu* ("give thanks") is said, as well as when *ana Adonai* is said. According to tradition, as the verse that begins with the word *hodu* has six words apart from the Divine name, each word is accompanied by a wave; and as the verse that begins with the phrase *ana Adonai* has three words except for the Divine name, each word is accompanied by two waves. While there are a myriad of homiletical reasons that explain the waving of the four species, the ritual recalls the agricultural theme of the festival by becoming an action-oriented prayer. The waving in all directions reflects the belief of the worshiper that God is everywhere.

During the *musaf* (additional) service, after the cantor has repeated the *amidah* prayer, an introductory hymn (which differs each day according to the calendar, taken from a series of hymns called *hoshanot* because they begin with the words *hosha na*) is read. The ark is then opened. The Torah is removed and the ark is left open. The reader takes the *lulav* and *etrog* and chants four introductory verses, each beginning with *hosha na*. Anyone in the congregation who has a *lulav* and *etrog* joins in a procession, repeating each verse with the reader. As *musaf* is generally not included in Reform congregations, this procession usually does not take place. Instead, it may take place during the Torah service itself. The waving of the *lulav* does not take place on the Sabbath. The rabbis feared that worshipers would carry their *lulavim* (plural) to the synagogue, a practice prohibited on the Sabbath. However, most Reform synagogues use the *lulav* in the synagogue on Shabbat.

On Hoshanah Rabbah (The Great Saving), seven circuits are made in the procession. During these prayers, the *lulav* and *etrog* are laid aside, and the *hoshanah*, which consists of five willow twigs tied together, is held. The willow was the symbol of the fruitfulness of rain, the amount of which was to be determined on the following day, Shemini Atzeret. At the end of the service, congregants strike the twigs against the ground. Most Reform congregations do not follow this practice. In modern times, the custom is to take the Torah scrolls from the ark and make seven circuits with them, singing short liturgical litanies, called *hoshanot*.

In the ancient Temple, the *lulav* was used only on the first day of the festival. Following the destruction of the Temple use of the *lulav* during the entire festival was mandated.

REFERENCES

Goodman, Philip. *The Sukkot and Simhat Torah Anthology*. Philadelphia: The Jewish Publication Society of America, 1973.
Isaacs, Ronald. *Every Person's Guide to Sukkot, Shemini Atzeret and Simchat Torah*. Northvale, NJ: Jason Aronson, 1999.
Strassfeld, Michael. *The Jewish Holidays: A Guide and Commentary*. New York: Harper & Row, Publishers, 1985.
Waskow, Arthur. *Seasons of Our Joy*. New York: Summit Books, 1986.

M

MAOT CHITTIN. Literally "wheat money," *maot chittin* is also known as *kimcha de-Pisha,* or flour for Passover. During Passover, in particular, care must be taken for the poor, because the costs for its observance may be greater than normal. Thus, the practice of distributing wheat money to meet the needs of the poor evolved. This gave rise to the development of special Passover funds in individual communities to meet the needs of its indigents.

REFERENCES

Goodman, Philip. *The Passover Anthology.* Philadelphia: The Jewish Publication Society of America, 1961.
Isaacs, Ronald. *Every Person's Guide to Passover.* Northvale, NJ: Jason Aronson, 1999.
Kamin, Ben. *Thinking Passover.* New York: Dutton, 1997.
Wolfson, Ron. *The Art of Jewish Living: The Passover Seder.* Woodstock, VT: Jewish Lights Publishing, 1996.

MATZAH. *Matzah* is the unleavened bread eaten on Passover when eating *chametz* (leavened products) is forbidden. It is forbidden to eat *matzah* on the day before Passover. However, it is customary to wait a longer period of time so that one may approach the first ***seder*** with a full and hearty appetite and be able to fulfill the commandment fully. The requirement to eat *matzah* is binding only on the first night of Passover, although the prohibition against eating *chametz* remains in effect throughout the festival (see Exodus 12:17). That is why special *matzah*, called *shemurah matzah* (literally unleavened bread that is watched), is eaten by many on the first night only and the special blessing over *matzah* is said only at the *seder*. Some eat only *shemurah matzah* during the entire festival.

In the preparation of *matzah*, bakers must take precautions during the kneading and baking process to make sure that the dough does not ferment and become leavened as a result. Some call this *matzah mitzvah*, meaning unleavened bread of the precept or commandment. A further precaution is taken for *shemurah matzah* during the harvesting and milling of the wheat that is to be used to make sure that rain or dampness does not cause fermentation.

REFERENCES

Goodman, Philip. *The Passover Anthology*. Philadelphia: The Jewish Publication Society of America, 1961.

Isaacs, Ronald. *Every Person's Guide to Passover*. Northvale, NJ: Jason Aronson, 1999.

Kamin, Ben. *Thinking Passover*. New York: Dutton, 1997.

Wolfson, Ron. *The Art of Jewish Living: The Passover Seder*. Woodstock, VT: Jewish Lights Publishing, 1996.

MEKHIRAT CHAMETZ. The selling of *chametz* (leavened products) on the morning of the first night of Passover, following the process of **biur chametz** (the burning of *chametz*). Only small quantities may be burned; large quantities must be sold (*mekhirat chametz*). In many communities, the rabbi "buys" the remaining *chametz* that might still be in one's home and then "sells" it or transfers ownership of it collectively to a non-Jew. This collective approach dates back to the early nineteenth century as a practical method for those in the food or liquor business, but was not fully accepted until late in the nineteenth century. The buyer has the right to take legal possession of it, but the physical transfer of the *chametz* is not made. This process was enacted to avoid financial loss from the (primarily commercial) destruction of large quantities of *chametz*. It also guarantees that no *chametz* will be in the "possession" or ownership of the household during the holiday. Because it is a complicated legal process, individuals usually designate the local rabbi to act as their agent for this transaction. Following Passover, the rabbi buys back the leaven and restores it to the possession of its original owners. The form of this sale changed over time. Today, it is technically a real sale. A price is set and a "down payment" is made. As the non-Jew does not want to pay the balance after Pesach, he returns it. It is a real sale in the sense that the buyer is permitted to consume the *chametz* during the holiday and may pay the purchase price should he or she choose to do so following Pesach.

Apparently, during the time of the Talmud, this was not a "legal fiction." Instead, the *chametz* was actually sold to a non-Jew as part of a normal business transaction. Thus, the practice emerged out of economic necessity rather than a convenience. Later, when Jews became involved in businesses such as the commercial production of alcoholic beverages, it became impossible actually to sell the products and have them removed. Thus, it became necessary to "sell" fermented products, which were not ready to be sold for consumption and could not be removed from the premises of the Jewish owner.

REFERENCES

Goodman, Philip. *The Passover Anthology*. Philadelphia: The Jewish Publication Society of America, 1961.
Isaacs, Ronald. *Every Person's Guide to Passover*. Northvale, NJ: Jason Aronson, 1999.
Kamin, Ben. *Thinking Passover*. New York: Dutton, 1997.
Wolfson, Ron. *The Art of Jewish Living: The Passover Seder*. Woodstock, VT: Jewish Lights Publishing, 1996.

MOURNER'S *KADDISH*. There are now five different types of the *kaddish* prayer. Originally, the *kaddish* was a doxology that was used to separate sections of the worship service and also at the conclusion of the study of rabbinic literature. Thus, its beginnings may more accurately be found in the house of study than in the synagogue. One *kaddish* is now reserved for mourners. We find the first mention of the practice of mourners reciting *kaddish* in the thirteenth century. However, this prayer was used to comfort mourners at the conclusion of *musaf* (additional service) some time earlier. A second expanded *kaddish* is said by some at the graveside interment. The prayer says nothing about death. Instead, it affirms a belief in God at a time, perhaps, when the individual feels most distant from and even abandoned by God.

A person who is in mourning for a parent must recite the *kaddish* at all public services, morning and evening, for eleven months. Originally, mourners recited *kaddish* for twelve months. However, as twelve months was the time allotted for the maximum period of punishment by the heavenly courts, the practice of a mourner saying *kaddish* for twelve months might be misinterpreted as if to say that one's parent deserved the maximum penalty. While this logic is no longer persuasive, the practice remains. However, some Reform rabbis still encourage the practice for twelve months. Some argue that stopping the daily reciting of kaddish at eleven months prepares the individual for observing **yahrzeit**, marking the anniversary of the death.

It was a former practice for people to say *kaddish* according to their standing in the community. Now mourners say *kaddish* together. In an effort to diminish the level of social visibility, the early Reform movement encouraged all its members to rise and join together to say *kaddish*. In the contemporary synagogue, this practice is in flux with a great variance in practice. Some encourage people to rise with those required to say *kaddish* and remain silent. Others are encouraged to say *kaddish* for those who have no survivors.

In each case, the reader of *kaddish* is required to take three steps backwards prior to its recitation. While its origin is unclear, some speculate that this practice is related to the practice of doing so prior to the recitation and following the conclusion of the *amidah* ("the standing prayer," the central prayer of the service). In this case, the individual uproots himself or herself from saying a prayer during which time he or she is supposed to be rooted (see Babylonian Talmud, Yoma 53b). In addition, the individual is taking leave of the Royal Presence of God. However, it is clear that the *kaddish*, in the traditional service, marks the end of the recitation of the *amidah* as much as it marks the transition from one section of the liturgy to another. By extension, the worshiper models this practice of taking leave each time *kaddish* is recited. The final paragraph of the *kaddish*, taken from the *amidah*, was added to reflect this practice.

When the *kaddish* is read at the conclusion of the funeral, Jewish law requires that the grave must be filled with earth before *kaddish* may be recited. However, most liberal Jews recite *kaddish* at the close of the funeral (or interment) regardless of how the body is disposed.

REFERENCES

Diament, Anita. *Saying Kaddish: How to Comfort the Dying, Bury the Dead, and Mourn as a Jew.* New York: Schocken Books, 1998.

Dobrinsky, Henry. *A Treasury of Sephardic Laws and Customs: The Ritual Practices of Syrian, Moroccan, Judeo-Spanish and Spanish and Portuguese Jews of North America*. Hoboken, NJ, and New York: KTAV and Yeshiva University Press, 1986.

Hauptman, Judith. "Death and Mourning: A Time for Weeping, A Time for Mourning." In *Celebration*, edited by Rela A. Geffen. Philadelphia: The Jewish Publication Society of America, 1993, pp. 226–251.

Kay, Alan A. *A Jewish Book of Comfort*. Northvale, NJ: Jason Aronson, 1996.

Lamm, Maurice. *The Jewish Way in Death and Mourning*. Middle Village, NY: Jonathan David Publishers, 1969.

Wieseltier, Leon. *Kaddish*. Alfred A. Knopf: New York: 1998.

N

NETILAT YADAYIM. The ritual of washing the hands upon rising in the morning and before meals is called *netilat yadayim*. Casual eating is distinguished from the eating of a regular meal by the eating of bread and the recital of **hamotzi**. This also warrants the recital of **birkat hamazon** following a meal. Before one eats bread, one washes one's hands ritually. The washing should be performed with a vessel and should result from human effort. Thus, holding one's hands under an open faucet does not satisfy this requirement. One must fill the vessel with water, hold it with the left hand, and pour it over the right hand. Then one should follow the same procedure with the other hand. This is repeated three times. After the hands are washed, one should recite the blessing, "Praised are You, Adonai our God, Sovereign of the Universe who makes us holy with *mitzvot* and instructs us concerning the washing of hands" as one dries them. As this ritual is connected to *hamotzi* and one is not supposed to interrupt the initiation of a blessing until its conclusion, it is customary not to speak until the bread has been eaten. While Orthodox Jews wash before each meal when bread is eaten, some Conservative Jews and few Reform and Reconstructionist Jews do so except perhaps on the Sabbath and holidays.

REFERENCES

Donin, Hayyim Halevy. *To Be a Jew: A Guide to Contemporary Observance*. New York: Basic Books, 1991.

Klein, Isaac. *A Guide to Jewish Religious Practice*. New York: The Jewish Theological Seminary of America, 1979.

P

PIDYON HABEN. Redemption of the firstborn (son) is achieved through the ritual of *pidyon haben*. This ceremony emerges from the following text: "The first issue of the womb of every being, human or animal, that is offered to Adonai shall be yours [that is, the priest's]; but you shall have the human firstborn redeemed, and you shall also have the firstling of animals redeemed. Take as their redemption price [for the human firstborn] from the age of one month up, the monetary equivalent of five shekels by the sanctuary weight, which is twenty *gerahs*" (Numbers 18: 15–16).

In the ancient world, the firstborn son had the specific responsibility of assisting the priest with his worship responsibilities. When the tabernacle was built in the wilderness, this vocation was transferred from the firstborn to the priestly tribe of Levi. As a result, parents became responsible for having their sons released from this obligation by redeeming their sons from a priest (*kohane*). This practice is recalled through the *pidyon haben* ceremony. However, members of the Jewish community probably maintained the ritual as an expressions of the joy following the birth of a child rather than for religious reasons. This was particularly true when elaborate celebrations following the **brit milah** were impractical.

According to Jewish law, in order to need to be redeemed, the firstborn must be a male and the first issue from the womb. Thus, he must be the firstborn to the mother, regardless of whether the father has had previous children. Births following miscarriage (after

40 days) or those delivered by Caesarean section do not have to be redeemed. The child of a *kohane* (priestly descendant) or Levite is also exempt.

The *pidyon haben* ceremony takes place on the child's thirty-first day unless it is a Sabbath or festival, in which case it is postponed to the next day. Unlike **brit milah**, *pidyon haben* may take place at night. In contemporary American practice, the *pidyon haben* is usually scheduled on the Sunday following the thirty-first day in order to encourage maximum attendance.

The ritual has four parts. First, the child is presented to the *kohane* (priestly descendant). Second, using a liturgical formula that mentions Passover and redemption, the father states his desire that the child be redeemed. Third, the father gives five shekel coins to the *kohane*. In return, the *kohane* accepts the coins and blesses the child, using the priestly benediction. In some communities, special coins are used. However, it is also common in the United States to use five silver dollars or Israeli shekels. Finally, guests enjoy a festive meal.

Because the Reform and Reconstructionist movements eliminated social class distinctions, most of their members do not engage in this ritual. In an effort to provide an equal opportunity ceremony for girls, some communities advocate an alternative ceremony called *kiddush peter rechem* (sanctifying the opening of the womb). In this case, the rabbi replaces the *kohane*. Both parents share in the ceremony, and money (often $18) is given to charity rather than to the officiant. Among liberal families who choose to participate in the more familiar *pidyon Haben* ceremony, mothers and fathers often share the responsibility equally.

REFERENCES

Diament, Anita. *The New Jewish Baby Book; Names, Ceremonies, and Customs: A Guide for Today's Families*. Woodstock, VT: Jewish Lights Publishing, 1994.

Diament, Anita, and Howard Cooper. *Living a Jewish Life*. New York: HarperCollins, 1996.

Golub, Mark, and Norman Cohen. "*Kiddush Peter Rehem*: An Alternative to Pidyon Haben." *CCAR Journal* vol. 20, no. 1 (Winter 1973): 71–78.

S

SEDER. Literally "order," the term *seder* refers to the (home-based) festive meal on the first two nights of Passover that follows a specific order. The *seder* grows out of an interpretation of Exodus 12:3–11 (the last meal the Israelites prepared before leaving Egypt) and from the prescription repeated four times urging the father to tell the story of the exodus to his children (Exodus 12: 26–27, 13:8, 13:14; Deuteronomy 6:20–21). The *seder* is divided into sections whose names emerge from the salient ritual element. By the admission of the rabbis, the *seder* follows the format of a Greek symposium and affords the participants of the *seder* to become the elite of the nobility, if only for a short period of time. The *seder* uses real food to concretize ideas.

The entire *seder* is to be conducted with participants in a comfortable (reclining, slouching) position, particularly while drinking. Like royalty rather than slaves, many people lean on a pillow during the *seder*. Generally, one leans to the left, which keeps the esophagus open and permits the individual to drink with the right hand. In some medieval Sephardic communities, people enhanced the reenactment of the *seder* by dressing for the journey. In order to add excitement to the contemporary *seder*, some choose to do similar things today, often adding readings of contemporary relevance. As a result, the *haggadah* (a book of narrative that takes participants through the story of the exodus during the *seder*), even in the most traditional communities, is quite flexible and responsive.

While the *seder* begins after sunset, there is some leniency among authorities to start the *seder* earlier should it be necessary to do so to accommodate young children. The table is set and the *seder* plate with symbolic elements is prepared. A shank bone (or a boiled beet if participants are vegetarian) is featured as the *zeroa* (literally, an arm outstretched to sow seed) to represent the sacrificial lamb. Alongside is a roasted egg, which represents the *chagigah*, a primitive springtime festival which the Israelites wanted the freedom to celebrate. Other elements are the bitter herb (usually horseradish) and a mildly bitter green, which is used to foreshadow the bitter herb and to encourage questions because of the odd nature of the ritual of dipping the vegetable in salt water before eating it. The green may also represent the spring and the salt (water) may represent the sea as the mother of life.

The *seder* follows a particular order (usually sung as a mnemonic device):

Kadesh: to make holy or separate; the **kiddush** is said over the first of four cups of wine (or grape juice). One is supposed to drink at least half the cup, which has been filled to overflowing. In some homes only the leader chants the *kiddush*. It is customary to stand while "making" *kiddush* and then sit while drinking.

Urchatz: washing; the *seder* continues with the washing of hands in a ritual manner without a blessing. This is done by pouring water over each one of one's hands, alternating two or three times. While there are a variety of explanations for washing, it is an old custom to wash prior to dipping food in liquid. No blessing is said, because no bread is to be eaten.

Karpas: greens; next greens, symbolic of spring, are eaten after they have been dipped in salt water. Some suggest that the dipping is done to encourage the curiosity of the children. This allows for the explanation: the salt water is symbolic of the slave's tears of bitterness. Some eat as much as half a potato. This is explained either as a means of counteracting the effect of drinking wine on an empty stomach or of satisfying one's hunger before the holiday meal is served. Others suggest that the choice to use *karpas* resulted from a play on words in the story of Joseph.

Yachatz: to break or divide; the middle of the three *matzot* on the table is divided in half. One half is left for the *afikomen* (an obscure Greek loan word that refers to the piece of **matzah** to be found and eaten as "dessert," which might mean "take out the sweets" or "remove the dishes" so that we can continue to celebrate or go elsewhere to celebrate). This is covered and hidden. In some communities, instead of sending off the children to find the *afikomen* later in the evening, they look for the opportunity to "steal" it and then offer it for "ransom" so that it can be shared as dessert. This was probably introduced to maintain the attention of the children throughout the *seder*. Yemenite Jews prohibited the "stealing" of the *afikomen*, because they considered it improper even to imitate the act of stealing.

Maggid: telling or narrating; the biblical story of the Passover is retold and is embellished by rabbinic commentary. The *seder* plate is lifted and the *matzot* are briefly uncovered. This signifies the beginning of the *haggadah*, the telling of the story, as this section makes up most of the *haggadah*. It contains well-known elements such as the four questions, the four sons, and the ten plagues. The section concludes with the second cup of wine.

Rachtzah: washing; this time, the hands are ritually washed, as they would before eating a meal that begins with the blessing over bread (or, in this case, *matzah*).

Motzi Matzah: "who brings forth *matzah*," namely God; this double blessing is said over the *matzah* just prior to the meal. Participants in the *seder* eat the *matzah* (only the top and middle of the three *matzot*).

Maror: bitter herbs; generally people eat horseradish (whose bitterness is sometimes mitigated by beet juice) with a blessing. Some dip the horseradish in *charoset* (a mixture of nuts, apples, and wine—and sometimes dates) to soften the taste and remind participants of the mortar used by the ancient Israelis in building for the Pharoah. Among Sephardim and Israelis, bitter lettuce, such as romaine, frequently is used for this purpose.

Korekh: participants eat a sandwich of sorts made of horseradish and *matzah*, using the bottom of the three *matzot*. This is called the Hillel sandwich and usually includes *charoset*.

Shulkhan Orekh: the meal is eaten, usually begun with a hard-boiled egg dipped in salt water. The egg is symbolic of the birth and renewal of spring.

Tzafun: the hidden; while there are different customs that surround the hunt for the hidden *afikomen*, it is eaten as dessert (the literal meaning of the word *afikomen*) after it is found.

Barekh: blessing; taking the form of grace after the meal, it is said over the third cup of wine.

Hallel: praise; the Hallel psalms are read and participants drink a fourth cup of wine. While some have already filled **Elijah's cup** of wine, many wait to do so until this time and then open the door for him. Elijah is to announce the coming of the Messiah. In the Middle Ages, Jewish tradition inserted a text of malediction against those who attempt to destroy the Jewish people. It emerged as a reaction to the violent persecution of the Jewish people that began with the Crusades. Some scholars suggest that *seder* participants opened their doors at this time to undermine the blood libel accusation.

Nirtzah: accepted; the *seder* concludes on a messianic note: "next year in Jerusalem." The singing continues and, on the second night of Passover, the first day of the *omer*, the period of time between Passover and Shavuot, is counted (*sefirat haomer*).

Some contemporary authorities argue for the addition of a fourth *matzah*, a *matzah* of hope for the oppressed communities—this began with the struggle to free Soviet Jewry—and a fifth cup of wine, which represents the hope potentially fulfilled in the founding of the modern state of Israel.

Recently, it has become common to conduct a variety of *sedarim* (plural of seder) in anticipation of the holiday, although they are not considered appropriate by traditional standards because one is not to eat *matzah* for a month in advance of the holiday so that the taste of unleavened bread should be fresh. Often these *sedarim* are designed for women (with the added expression of Miriam's cup to symbolize and capture the expressed role of women in the struggle for freedom). Others are interfaith *sedarim*, which celebrate community cooperation and foster interfaith relations. In addition, many synagogues hold community *sedarim* on the second night of the holiday.

As other holidays, the Reform movement rejected the need for the two-day celebration that introduces and concludes the full Passover holiday. Thus, it only celebrated the *seder* on the first day of Passover rather than on the first and second. However, over the past decade, increasing numbers of Reform congregations also sponsor second-day community *sedarim*.

Tu Bishevat *Seder*

In an effort to deepen the observance of Tu Bishevat, many communities have borrowed from a mystical tradition and established a *seder* for this holiday. This tradition originally made its way out of Safed and into the general Jewish community by oral tradition alone until it was written down in the seventh century in a compendium called *Chemdat Yamim*. Because some people incorrectly speculated that the false messiah Shabbatai Tzvi prepared the volume, members of the Jewish community shunned many of the practices the volume celebrated. However, as a result of the attractive nature of some of the rituals, they were republished separately as *Pri Etz Hadar*. This provoked greater use of the *seder*. The entire practice emerged from the belief that the Tree of Life is also renewed on Tu Bishevat.

As there is no fixed ritual for the Tu Bishevat *seder*, a variety of rituals can be found. In most cases, the meal includes spring fruits from Israel and varieties of grape juice. This probably emerged from the celebrations in central and eastern Europe during which time communities sang Psalm 104 and the fifteen psalms of ascent (120–134). These psalms were sung as the Levites ascended the fifteen steps to the inner court of the Israelites in the ancient Temple. Corresponding to these psalms was the custom to eat fifteen kinds of fruit, especially some from the land of Israel, including olives, dates, grapes, figs, and pomegranates. A special association eventually arose with carob, as this is the tree that—according to legend—sustained Rabbi Shimon bar Yochai as he hid from the Romans in a cave.

In one version of the *seder* ritual, there are three courses made up, respectively, of fruits that have no shell, fruits with an inedible inner pit, and fruits with a tough outer shell. These represent three of the four processes of creation. The structure of the fruit represents the kind of protection needed during each individual process. First is *asiyah*, or action, the physical world that surrounds us. Second is *yetzirah*, or foundation, the level in which the ideal version of our world is set. Third is *beriah*, or creation, in which the inner dynamic processes that result in forms are set in motion. The last process is *atzilut*, or emanation. Here God infuses the processes with their initial life. This process is thought to be beyond representation by the fruit. Within each category of fruit are ten different species of fruit to be eaten during the *seder*. Saying blessings over the fruit releases the holy sparks that they contain. Through the process of gematria, the mystics argue that chewing the fruit has a more profound effect.

The kabbalistic *seder* includes drinking four cups of wine. First is a cup of white wine, then white mixed with a little red (to make pink), then white mixed with a lot of red (deep rose), then red with a drop of white in it. These may represent the seasons, or they may represent the four letters of God's name. The *seder* also includes readings from sacred literature on trees and fruit. In addition to the practice of a Tu Bishevat *seder*, some communities have augmented this idea and developed a similar *seder* for Yom Ha-atzmaut (Israel Independence Day).

REFERENCES

Birnbaum, Philip. *A Book of Jewish Concepts*. New York: Hebrew Publishing Co., 1975.

Goodman, Philip. *The Passover Anthology*. Philadelphia: The Jewish Publication Society of America, 1961.
Greenberg, Irving. *The Jewish Way: Living the Holidays*. New York: Summit Books, 1988.
Isaacs, Ronald. *Every Person's Guide to Passover*. Northvale, NJ: Jason Aronson, 1999.
Kamin, Ben. *Thinking Passover*. New York: Dutton, 1997.
Strassfeld, Michael. *The Jewish Holidays: A Guide and Commentary*. New York: Harper & Row, 1985.
Waskow, Arthur I. *Seasons of Our Joy: A Handbook of Jewish Festivals*. New York: Summit Books, 1986.
Wolfson, Ron. *The Art of Jewish Living: The Passover Seder*. Woodstock, VT: Jewish Lights Publishing, 1996.

SEFIRAT HAOMER. Literally "counting the *omer*," this occurs in the period between Pesach (Passover) and Shavuot. The *omer* refers to an offering brought to the Temple on the sixteenth of Nisan, thus giving the name to this period. Historically, this was a time of anxious waiting, the interval between the barley and wheat harvests. In Leviticus 23:9ff, we are taught, "when you enter the land which I am giving you and reap its harvest, you shall bring the first sheaf (*omer*) of your harvest to the priest ... the priest shall wave it on the day after the Sabbath [the rabbis read this Sabbath as Pesach]." In the *sefirat haomer* ritual, the priest took the offering in his outstretched hands and moved it from side to side, then up and down. After the waving, a burnt offering was made, as well as an offering of flour and a libation of water. Afterwards, it was permissible to eat of the new harvest.

According to the Talmud, the rabbis interpreted the ceremony as a prayer to God for the protection of the harvest from damaging winds and other calamities (Babylonian Talmud, Menachot 62a). The specific timing of the *omer* was mired in great debate during the Temple period, a reflection of the struggle for community authority between the priests and the rabbis. The Sadducean priests (and continued by the Karaites) interpreted the "Sabbath" in Leviticus 23 to refer to the first Sabbath after Passover. Thus, this forced Shavuot to always fall on a Sunday. Similarly, the Jews of Ethiopia interpreted it to mean the day after Passover is over. Thus, they observe Shavuot six days later than the rest of the Jewish community.

Once the *omer* offering was discontinued following the destruction of the Temple, the rabbis invited the community to count (*lis-por*; *sefirah*) the 49 days. Because of the similarity between this Hebrew word for counting and the word that describes the mystical emanation of God (likewise *sefirah*), the mystics developed a matrix for seven of these emanations; they applied one of them to each of the weeks of the *omer* and one, again, to each day within each week. Thus, the counting was given a mystical character. Counting in this way provides the entire period with a psychospiritual quality.

This short ritual of counting takes place after sunset, following the evening service, from the second day of Passover until Shavuot. Worshipers remain standing, and generally, a meditation is read (although it is not required). Then Psalm 67 is recited (although it, too, is not required). A prayer often follows before the specific blessing for counting is recited. Next, a specific formula for counting is used, which includes the day and then a restatement of the accumulation of weeks and days. For example, the twelfth day would be marked as follows: "Today is the twelfth day of the *omer*, one week and five days." Among some Sephardic communities, people do not work from sunset to dawn during the *omer* period. Among others, women do not work at all during the entire *omer* season.

On the thirty-third day of the *omer* period, the Jewish community is offered a bit of a respite. The day is called Lag B'omer, literally the thirty-third day (from the alphanumeric) of the *omer*. This day may have emerged from the desire for a relaxation from the angst-filled harvest season. Or perhaps it emerged out of the mourning for the Temple. Possibly it developed from the deadly epidemic that threatened Rabbi Akiva's students (or soldiers) during the second century C.E. It may even have been borrowed from the spring mourning period of the Romans during which time souls wandered on earth and marriages were prohibited. Some also say that it is the anniversary of the death of Rabbi Simon bar Yochai, to whom the writing of the *Zohar* is ascribed.

While most congregations move through this ritual rather quickly, there is a trend in some congregations to embellish the ritual. In addition, the designation of Yom Ha-atzmaut (Israel Independence Day) and Yom Hashoah (Holocaust Remembrance Day) has changed the entire tone of the period. Most Reform congregations do not count the *omer*. However, as is the case with many rituals, the Reform movement is reevaluating the place of counting the *omer* even if its members do not resonate entirely with the foundation for the ritual.

During the period of the *omer* (except on Lag B'omer), time takes on the nuances of mourning. However, the specific timing of this "mourning" differs among communities. Generally, weddings are avoided. Haircuts are prohibited and public celebrations are generally discouraged. In the mid-1980s, the Rabbinical Assembly Law Committee (Conservative) ruled against the prohibition of marriages and other mourning practices—except for the weekend before Yom Hashoah—because of the unclear origin of these prohibitions. Likewise, Reform rabbis will officiate at weddings during the period of the *omer*. The traditional community continues to maintain the *omer* prohibitions, but the liberal community generally has not. Parallel to the counting of the *omer*, many traditional Jews study *Pirke Avot* on the Sabbath afternoons of this season.

REFERENCES

Donin, Hayyim Halevy. *To Be a Jew: A Guide to Contemporary Observance.* New York: Basic Books, 1991.

Greenberg, Irving. *The Jewish Way: Living the Holidays.* New York: Summit Books, 1988.

Isaacs, Ronald. *Every Person's Guide to Passover.* Northvale, NJ: Jason Aronson, 1999.

Klein, Isaac. *A Guide to Jewish Religious Practice.* New York: The Jewish Theological Seminary of America, 1979.

Olitzky, Kerry M., with Rachel Smookler. *Anticipating Revelation: An Omer Calendar for the Spirit.* New York: Synagogue 2000, 1998.

Strassfeld, Michael. *The Jewish Holidays: A Guide and Commentary.* New York: Harper & Row, 1985.

SEUDAH SHELISHIT. Literally "the third meal," this term refers to the third of three meals considered to be commanded by God as part of the observance and celebration of the Sabbath. The obligation to eat three meals is based on an understanding of Exodus 16:25 in which the word "today" is repeated three times. It is eaten after the afternoon worship service, *mincha*. It is a light dairy meal, because at this point in the Sabbath, observers of the Sabbath are not as interested in physical sustenance as they are in spiritual nourishment. **Kiddush** is not said, but two loaves of *challah* are used. The mood is yearning and longing. Sabbath observers become aware of their potential to actually bring the Messiah. The *zemirot* (table songs) are slow and repetitive with many references to the Messiah. *Divrei Torah* (literally "words of Torah," or Torah teaching; see **Devar Torah**) are generally spoken, often through the teaching of *Pirke Avot* or Psalms, depending on the season. In the Hasidic community, disciples would spend hours at the rabbi's table (*tish*). The *seudah shelishit* is common to most Orthodox and Conservative and some Reconstructionist synagogues. However, it is a relatively uncommon feature of Reform synagogues.

REFERENCES

Kaplan, Aryeh. *Sabbath: Day of Eternity*. New York: National Conference of Synagogue Youth/Union of Orthodox Jewish Congregations of America, 1982.
Klein, Isaac. *A Guide to Jewish Religious Practice*. New York: The Jewish Theological Seminary of America, 1979.
Millgram, Abraham Ezra. *Sabbath: Day of Delight*. Philadelphia: The Jewish Publication Society of America, 1944.
Shapiro, Mark Dov. *Gates of Shabbat*. New York: Central Conference of American Rabbis, 1991.
Wolfson, Ron. *The Shabbat Seder*. Woodstock, VT: Jewish Lights Publishing, 1996.

SEVEN DAYS OF FEASTING. While sometimes this is also called *sheva berakhot*, it more specifically refers to the seven days of festive meals prepared and presented by friends and family following a wedding. According to tradition, at least ten people were necessary for the celebration, which would enable the full recitation of *birkat hamazon*. When at least one new person joins the celebration, the seven wedding blessings (also called *sheva berakhot*) are repeated in the context of *birkat hamazon*.

These seven days correspond to the seven days of mourning (*shiva*). Both are considered times of transition when community support is necessary, particularly at a time when it was thought that individuals were vulnerable to evil spirits. In the context of planned marriages, the community helped the couple through the initial phase of anxiety that followed the wedding.

According to traditional Jewish law, seven days of feasting are required when a man marries a virgin; only three days of feasting are required when the woman is a divorcee or widow. The book of Judges refers to the seven days of feasting when Samson was married. Thus, some scholars assume that this aspect of the marital celebration dates back to biblical times.

The modern honeymoon has displaced this form of celebration in many communities. With the mobile society, families have become far flung. Thus, some people celebrate these *sheva berakhot* on the road, often taking the form of a special **kiddush** or **aliyah**.

REFERENCES

Diament, Anita. *The New Jewish Wedding*. New York: Summit Books, 1985.
Goodman, Philip and Hanna. *The Jewish Marriage Anthology*. Philadelphia: The Jewish Publication Society of America, 1965.
Routtenberg, Lilly S., and Ruth R. Seldin. *The Jewish Wedding Book*. New York: Schocken Books, 1967.

SHALOM ZAKHAR. Literally "welcome to the male" (alternatively *ben zakhar*), this medieval celebration of welcoming a son on the first Friday night after his birth evolved into an enduring custom. (Because of the grammatical construction of the phrase [called *smichut*], the ritual should be called *shelom zakhar*). The original ceremony emerged from an obscure festivity mentioned in the Talmud under the name *yeshua haben*, "the salvation of a son" (Babylonian Talmud, Baba Kamma 80a). While the commentator Rashi (1040–1105) identified this with **pidyon haben**, Rabbenu Tam (1100–1171) disagreed and, instead, argued that it was a celebration that followed the birth of a male child. It is possible that it arose when *yeshua haben* was discontinued and perhaps prohibited.

The ceremony usually takes place on the first Friday evening following the birth of a boy or during the evening just prior to the circumcision. It expresses joy over the birth following the text, "as soon as a male comes into the world, peace comes into the world" (Babylonian Talmud, Niddah 31b). During the evening, the *shema* (the basic statement of Jewish faith, said in morning and evening prayers as well as prior to retiring at night) is recited, as is Genesis 48:16, along with some psalms and other prayers.

Among Oriental Jews, this ceremony is called *shasha* or *blada*. In those communities, special portions of aggadic literature are read from a booklet called *berit olam*, which honors the prophet Elijah. It is customary to serve boiled chick peas, because of a word play on the word that reflects God's promise to Abraham (Genesis 22:17). In addition, lentils (a symbol of mourning) are served, because the family mourns the loss of Torah knowledge that, according to rabbinic legend, the child possessed in the womb and lost as part of the birthing process. Some communities, particularly liberal ones, observe the ritual simply for coffee and dessert.

REFERENCES

Diament, Anita. *The New Jewish Baby Book; Names, Ceremonies, and Customs: A Guide for Today's Families*. Woodstock, VT: Jewish Lights Publishing, 1994.

Diament, Anita, and Howard Cooper. *Living a Jewish Life*. New York: HarperCollins, 1996.

SHELOSHIM. Literally "thirty," *sheloshim* refer to the first 30 days of mourning, reckoned from the interment and including the seven days of **shiva**. After the *shiva* period, the mourner returns to a normal routine, but a number of mourning customs initiated during *shiva* are continued during the rest of *sheloshim*. Specifically, while one may return to conjugal marital relations, one is to avoid forms of entertainment. The mourner returns to work but continues to say the **mourner's kaddish** in the context of a daily *minyan*. During the second week of mourning, an individual is not supposed to sit in his or her regular seat in the synagogue. However, as most synagogues today, particularly in the Reform, Reconstructionist, and Conservative movements, no longer have fixed seating, this is not observed. Technically, *sheloshim* ends the full mourning period for all relatives except those grieving a parent. Festivals affect *sheloshim* in a variety of ways.

Among Sephardic Jews, the final weekend before the end of the *sheloshim* period is marked by a reading of a selection of the *Zohar* following the afternoon service in a fashion similar to the conclusion of *shiva*. This is followed by the evening service, a eulogy, and a sweet table. Following *sheloshim*, members of the family gather at the cemetery—in the same way they did to conclude *shiva*—and recite verses of Psalm 119 that spell out the name of the deceased.

REFERENCES

Diament, Anita. *Saying Kaddish: How to Comfort the Dying, Bury the Dead, and Mourn as a Jew*. New York: Schocken Books, 1998.

Dobrinsky, Henry. *A Treasury of Sephardic Laws and Customs: The Ritual Practices of Syrian, Moroccan, Judeo-Spanish and Spanish and Portuguese Jews of North America*. Hoboken, NJ, and New York: KTAV and Yeshiva University Press, 1986.

Hauptman, Judith. "Death and Mourning: A Time for Weeping, A Time for Mourning." In *Celebration*, edited by Rela A. Geffen. Philadelphia: The Jewish Publication Society of America, 1993, pp. 226–251.

Kay, Alan A. *A Jewish Book of Comfort*. Northvale, NJ: Jason Aronson, 1996.

Lamm, Maurice. *The Jewish Way in Death and Mourning*. Middle Village, NY: Jonathan David Publishers, 1969.

Wieseltier, Leon. *Kaddish*. Alfred A. Knopf: New York: 1998.

SHEMIRAH. The word *shemirah* is the equivalent of the English phrase "guard duty." It refers to the responsibility to watch over or guard the body of a deceased person. Jewish law requires that a body is never left alone. In the ancient world, guards (*shomrim*) protected the body from scavengers and thieves. The *shomer* (guardian of respect) is exempt from all religious obligations during the period of *shemirah*. If there are two *shomrim*, one discharges his religious duties in another room while the other watches over the body. When this reason became irrelevant, particularly in the modern period, *shomrim* guarded the body to protect it from disrespect and indifference.

It is preferable that friends and members of the family take on the responsibility of *shemirah*. According to traditional Jewish law, men may only serve as *shomrim* for deceased men and women may only serve as *shomrot* for deceased women. Whether the *shomrim* are men or women, they accompany the body from the home or hospital to the mortuary. There they take turns until the funeral (and interment). This is considered to be a fulfillment of a *mitzvah* that is *chesed shel emet* (a truly merciful act) because the deceased can never repay the individual for his or her deed of lovingkindness. While in the presence of the deceased, those doing *shemirah* read psalms, particularly Psalm 23 ("The Lord is my shepherd; I shall not want") and Psalm 91, which describes God as One who consoles, protects, and redeems.

In many communities, activities surrounding death and mourning are handled by the *chevra kaddisha* (burial society). While members of many communities still take on the responsibility of *shemirah*, as might be expected, today funeral homes offer the services of *shomrim* on a fee-for-service basis. Among liberal Jews, the practice of *shemirah* is largely disregarded. Most funeral homes are staffed twenty-four hours a day. Thus, the body is technically never alone. In addition, as bodies are refrigerated until burial, *shomrim* are unable actually to sit next to the body of the deceased and watch over it.

REFERENCES

Diament, Anita. *Saying Kaddish: How to Comfort the Dying, Bury the Dead, and Mourn as a Jew.* New York: Schocken Books, 1998.
Hauptman, Judith. "Death and Mourning: A Time for Weeping, A Time for Mourning." In *Celebration*, edited by Rela A. Geffen. Philadelphia: The Jewish Publication Society of America, 1993, pp. 226–251.
Lamm, Maurice. *The Jewish Way in Death and Mourning.* Middle Village, NY: Jonathan David Publishers, 1969.
Wieseltier, Leon. *Kaddish*. Alfred A. Knopf: New York: 1998.

SHEVA BERAKHOT. Literally "seven blessings," this refers to the set of blessings offered during a wedding by a rabbi or others who are given the honor. *Sheva berakhot* also sometimes refers to the **seven days of feasting**, or festive meals that are given by friends and family for seven days following the wedding. Because these blessings are incorporated into ***birkat hamazon***, these receptions are often referred to as *sheva berakhot*. Jewish tradition also calls the seven blessings *birkhot chattanim*, or "groom's blessings." A presence of a *minyan* is required to recite these blessings. While the groom is not supposed to recite these blessings—as they are designed for the bride and groom—he may recite them should no one else be able to do. These blessings encompass a variety of themes: the creation of the world and of humanity and the happiness of the couple and of humanity. Through these blessings, the state of marriage is placed into a dynamic relationship with the beginning and end of Jewish history: Eden and the Messianic Era.

The initial three blessings do not refer to the marriage at all. Instead, they provide the foundation for the blessings that follow. The final blessing is a climax of rejoicing, with a listing of ten synonyms for joy that culminates with praise for God, who nurtures the happiness of bride and groom. The Talmud mentions only six blessings. A seventh blessing, the ***kiddush***, was added at the beginning as a way of rounding the number to seven, which has greater mystical significance. The seven blessings follow:

1. "Praised are You, Adonai our God, Sovereign of the universe who created fruit of the vine." This blessing is read first when it is recited under the ***chuppah***. It is read last when it is part of *birkat hamazon*, following the festive meal of celebration. If the reading of these blessings is shared by

a group of people, it is customary for the one who reads this first blessing also to read the one that follows.

2. "Praised are You, Adonai our God, Sovereign of the universe who has created everything for Your glory." This is the only context in which this praise of God is offered.

3. "Praised are You, Adonai our God, Sovereign of the universe, creator of humankind."

4. "Praised are You, Adonai our God, Sovereign of the universe, who created humankind after Your likeness, in Your image and has prepared a perpetual fabric for humans out of God's own self. Praised are You, Adonai creator of humankind." This blessing refers to the human ability to procreate and imitate the eternality of God.

5. "May she who was barren be exceedingly glad and rejoice when her children are united in her midst in joy. Praised are You, Adonai who makes Zion joyful through her children." Zion is the guest at every wedding who celebrates the joy of her children and the perpetual renewal of the Jewish people.

6. "O make these beloved companions greatly rejoice even as You rejoiced Your creation in the Garden of Eden as of old. Praised are You, Adonai, who causes bride and groom to rejoice."

7. "Praised are You, Adonai our God, Sovereign of the universe, who created joy and gladness, bridegroom and bride, mirth and exultation, pleasure and delight, love, brotherhood, peace and fellowship. Soon may there be heard in the cities of Judah and in the streets of Jerusalem, the voice of joy and gladness, the voice of the groom and the bride, the jubilant voice of grooms from their bridal canopies and of youths from their feasts of song. Praised are You, Adonai who causes the groom to rejoice with the bride." This last blessing, which is actually a form of petition, is the only one that may be recited at the table after a meal and during the seven days of feasting following the wedding, without the presence of a *minyan* but with a minimum of three participants. It serves as a summary of the themes in the previous blessings. Following this seventh blessing, bride and groom sip the wine.

REFERENCES

Diament, Anita. *The New Jewish Wedding*. New York: Summit Books, 1985.

Goodman, Philip and Hanna. *The Jewish Marriage Anthology*. Philadelphia: The Jewish Publication Society of America, 1965.

Routtenberg, Lilly S., and Ruth R. Seldin. *The Jewish Wedding Book*. New York: Schocken Books, 1967.

SHIVA. Literally "seven," the term refers to the first seven days of mourning, beginning with the day in which interment takes place. However, a death on the first day of a major festival (Passover, Shavuot, Sukkot) can delay *shiva* until the conclusion of the festival. Moreover, the onset of a major festival brings the *shiva* period to an end regardless of how many days have elapsed. A wedding celebration may also change the effect of the laws of mourning.

Shiva is divided into two parts. The first three days following interment are a period of intense grief. (Hence, some Reform and Reconstructionist rabbis have abbreviated *shiva* to this period only.) During this period, mourners are required to remain at home (except to go to the synagogue for Sabbath, at which time they enter following the introductory **kabbalat Shabbat** [welcoming the Sabbath] liturgy). (This is not the case in most Reform synagogues due to the abbreviation of liturgy and the desire not to single out mourners.) Friends are encouraged to visit ("to make a *shiva* call") throughout the week. The last four days of the week make up the second part of *shiva*.

During *shiva*, it is customary to refrain from work and commerce unless there is a clearly articulated public need or the mourners are very poor. Among more traditional Jews, shaving (or haircutting of any sort) is avoided, as is personal grooming (except for hygienic purposes). New clothes are not to be worn and one should refrain from conjugal marital relations. The formal study of Torah is prohibited as well, but mourners are encouraged to reflect on books of the Bible, such as Psalms and Job.

The Central Conference of American Rabbis, the central professional organization of Reform rabbis, decided in 1890 to discontinue most of the traditional customs related to mourning. These included the tearing of garments, causing the beard to grow, sitting on the floor, removing leather shoes, and the prohibition of washing, bathing, and greeting. However, some Reform Jews chose to observe these customs nonetheless. Recently, many Reform Jews have reclaimed these customs.

Certain *shiva* practices are to be done immediately upon returning from the cemetery. First, traditionally one ritually washes one's hands. It is an ancient custom to cleanse when leaving the presence of death to rid oneself of the impurities associated with it. Second, mourners eat a meal of consolation prepared for them by friends. This ensures that they will not deprive themselves of nourishment because of their grief. During *shiva*, mourners sit lower than others, usually on low stools; traditionally, they do not wear shoes with leather soles (a former sign of comfort and luxury).

During *shiva*, a candle, which lasts throughout the seven-day period, is kindled immediately upon entering the house of *shiva* following the funeral. There are differences of opinion as to where the candle should be placed, but it should be in the home of the deceased or wherever *shiva* is being observed.

While the practice of covering (or clouding over) of mirrors in a house of mourning has been customary for a long time, it is unclear how this custom developed. As a result, there are various reasons for wanting to do so, including: (1) Human beings are made in the image of God. As that image is diminished in the face of death, human images reflected in the mirror should be symbolically diminished through the covering of the mirror; (2) Mourners should focus on their relationship with the deceased and not on personal vanity; (3) The great appeal of mirrors, especially of those that are ornate or unusually decorated, should not draw anyone's attention away from the responsibility of mourning or of comforting the mourner; (4) Finally, the mirror reflects the image of individuals. Mirrors are not permitted in the deceased's home, because it is transformed into a house of worship during *shiva*.

At the conclusion of *shiva*, mourners "get up" and walk a short distance, usually around the block, to symbolize their return to society and the real world, from which death had forced them to withdraw. Historically, some Jews ended *shiva* by sewing up the tear in the garment (***keriah***), depending on their relationship to the deceased. Others went to the gravesite.

Among Sephardic Jews, the conclusion of *shiva* is marked by a reading that takes place at the final afternoon service, at which time a selection from the *Zohar* is read. Words of eulogy are again offered by the rabbi, followed by a dinner for the mourners and all who are present. This same ceremony is repeated on the weekend before the thirty days of **sheloshim** have passed. The following morning, family members join together at the cemetery and recite selections of Psalm 119 that spell out the name of the deceased. A member of the *chevra kaddisha* (burial society) washes the hands of family members as they leave the cemetery and then breaks the vessel that held the water, a symbolic gesture suggesting that death should not visit the household again.

REFERENCES

Diament, Anita. *Saying Kaddish: How to Comfort the Dying, Bury the Dead, and Mourn as a Jew*. New York: Schocken Books, 1998.

Dobrinsky, Henry. *A Treasury of Sephardic Laws and Customs: The Ritual Practices of Syrian, Moroccan, Judeo-Spanish and Spanish and Portuguese Jews of North America*. Hoboken, NJ, and New York: KTAV and Yeshiva University Press, 1986.

Hauptman, Judith. "Death and Mourning: A Time for Weeping, A Time for Mourning." In *Celebration*, edited by Rela A. Geffen. Philadelphia: The Jewish Publication Society of America, 1993, pp. 226–251.

Kay, Alan A. *A Jewish Book of Comfort*. Northvale, NJ: Jason Aronson, 1996.

Lamm, Maurice. *The Jewish Way in Death and Mourning*. Middle Village, NY: Jonathan David Publishers, 1969.

Wieseltier, Leon. *Kaddish*. Alfred A. Knopf: New York: 1998.

T

TAHARA. This term means "cleansing" or "purification" and refers to the physical preparation of the body through ceremonial washing of the dead prior to a burial. This act is considered one of the highest *mitzvot* (commandments) because it cannot be repaid. Traditional scholars suggest that the ritual responds to Ecclesiastes 5:15, "As he came, he shall go." The ritual of *tahara* is not mentioned in the Bible. However, communities used sweet-smelling spices when they buried kings, according to I Chronicles 16:14. There are also baths located below the Tombs of the Kings in Jerusalem, which were used either for cleansing the dead or for rituals performed by priests.

Tahara is a communal acknowledgement that every individual is made in the image of God and thus should be treated as such—in death as in life. Men perform *tahara* for male members of the community and women perform it for women. Families members do not participate. During the washing and the *tahara*, the father-in-law, mother's husband, and brother-in-law of the deceased may not be present, according to the traditional Jewish law. The females in a similar relationship may not be present during the *tahara* of a woman.

Usually, members of the local *chevra kaddisha* (literally "holy society," generally translated as burial society) do the ceremonial washing of the body; in some communities, staff members from the local funeral home prepare the bodies. The *chevra kaddisha* is a voluntary group of anonymous men and women who have studied the laws of this ritual and learned its practice by watching others with more experience. It is desirable that at least four, preferably five, people participate. Communities differ with respect to the customs of the *chevra kaddisha*. Attendants (called *mit'assekim*) lay the body on a special board (referred to as a *tahara* board) with the feet of the deceased toward the door. This position symbolizes the escape of the impurity. Attendants use water to transform the ritual state of the body from impure to pure. This parallels the immersion into the *mikvah* (ritual bath) for the purpose of personal transformation (see *tevilah*). The attendants begin by washing their hands in the same ritual manner as one does upon waking or before saying **hamotzi** prior to eating bread (see **netilat yadayim**). Then attendants undress the body. Next they thoroughly rub and cleanse the body with lukewarm water. They comb the hair and cut and clean fingernails and toenails. The order of the washing is as follows: first the entire head, then the neck, the right hand, the right upper half of the body, the right lower half of the body, the right foot, the left hand, the left upper half of the body, the left lower half of the body, and the left foot. The body is then inclined on its left side and the right side of the back is washed in the same order. The body is then inclined on its right side and the left side of the back is washed. To protect the modesty of the individual, attendants expose individual body parts as they wash them. The blood that flows at death may not be washed away. Other blood, such as from a wound, may be washed. If the individual died violently or by an accident and blood is splattered over the body, no *tahara* is performed.

Members of the *chevra kaddisha* wash their hands once again. Then these attendants pour "nine measures," or *kavim* (about 24 quarts), of water over the entire body while holding the body in a standing position with the head upright. They pour the water as a steady stream: two members take a pail of water with a minimum of 12 quarts and pour it; then two other members follow suit. Some straw or wood is placed under the feet. This process is the central and essential part of the *tahara*. If it is not possible to hold the body upright (because an insufficient number of the *chevra kaddisha* are present), then available members raise the body on several pieces of wood and pour water over the entire body. Afterwards—in either case—attendants say three times: *tahor hu* (he is pure) or *tahor hee* (she is pure). While the water is being poured, other members dry the *tahara* board. Then they dry the body thoroughly and dress it in simple white shrouds, placing the body back on the *tahara* board.

While generally there is equality about rituals related to death, the rite of *tahara* for great rabbis and scholars is more elaborate. Some communities actually immerse the body in a *mikvah*. Following the preparation of the body, attendants wash their hands in salted water. During *tahara*, other attendants recite biblical verses, such as Zechariah 3:4, Ezekiel 36:25, and Song of Songs 5:11. In some traditional communities, attendants next rub the front of the body and the head with a beaten egg. Some use the white of a raw egg mixed with a little wine or vinegar. Others use the mixture only to wash the head. This symbolizes the continuous cycle of life.

The *tahara* should take place as close to the funeral and interment as possible, preferably within three hours. When this is not possible—such as during the summer—attendants should be careful that the shrouds do not get soiled prior to the burial.

The *chevra kaddisha* does its work quietly and in somber tones. While the process begins with a prayer called *Hamol*, which asks God to forgive the deceased, it concludes with each individual member of the *chevra kaddisha* asking the deceased for forgiveness for any act of disrespect he or she might have performed.

In the past, traditional cemeteries had special rooms for *tahara*. Now members of the community perform *tahara* either in the hospital or in a mortuary. Most Reform Jews do not observe this ritual. However, some congregations have established their own burial societies to provide *tahara* for those members who desire it.

REFERENCES

Diament, Anita. *Saying Kaddish: How to Comfort the Dying, Bury the Dead, and Mourn as a Jew*. New York: Schocken Books, 1998.

Lamm, Maurice. *The Jewish Way in Death and Mourning*. Middle Village, NY: Jonathan David Publishers, 1969.

TALLIT. This term is generally used to the refer to the large prayer shawl (*tallit gadol*) worn during morning prayers rather than the *tallit katan* (small *tallit*), also known as *arba kanfot* (four corners), a four-cornered undergarment with a **tzitzit** on each corner. The basic command for the use of a fringed garment comes from the Torah: "You should see them [the fingers] and remember all the commandments of God" (Numbers 15:39). From this verse, the rabbis drew the conclusion that the fingers should be visible; thus, they should be worn only in the daytime. The worshiper puts on the *tallit* and **tefillin** before beginning morning prayers and wears them for the morning and additional *musaf* service. The exception is the morning of Tisha B'av when they are not worn and the afternoon of Tisha B'av when they are worn. In addition, the *tallit* is worn during the Kol Nidre service on the evening of Yom Kippur. While Moses ibn Machir, in his *Seder Hayom*, defended the wearing of *tallit* and *tefillin* during the afternoon service, the general practice of wearing *tallit* was limited to the service reader (without saying the blessing). Moreover, even the service leader should not wear it if it is near dark, according to Judah Eisenstein (1854–1956) in his *Otzar Dinim Uminhagim*. The Sephardim (Jews originally of Spanish origin) nevertheless, seem to rely more heavily on the position of *Seder Hayom* (the book through which much of Lurianic Kabbalah came into liturgical practice). The difference might be attributed to the common practice of Ashkenazim (from the medieval term for Germany, referring to those Jews whose ancestors are from Central and Eastern Europe) of reciting the afternoon service just before the evening service.

The practice of the reader wearing the *tallit* on Friday evening probably arose as a way of making his responsibility to the congregation, particularly to lead *kaddish*. It was transferred to the rabbi because of his role as teacher or preacher to the congregation. This custom appears to have been in flux in the seventh century but was clearly established by the eighteenth century.

Recognizing that traditional Jewish boys and men wear the *tallit katan*, there are variations in community custom regarding the age at which a man begins wearing the *tallit*. In ancient communities, garments were four-cornered and the *tzitzit* was attached directly to it. In order to prevent the obsolescence of this practice, the prayer shawl was designed. In some communities, all male worshipers wear the *tallit*. Some start at the age of thirteen (*bar mitzvah* age). In other communities, only married men wear the *tallit*. However, even unmarried men will put on a *tallit* for an **aliyah**. In most American synagogues, men over the age of thirteen wear the *tallit*. The *tallit* is also traditionally worn by the bridegroom and placed on the body of the deceased over the shroud.

While the practice has been observed in Orthodox, Conservative, and Reconstructionist congregations, many Reform Jews historically refrained from donning the *tallit*. In recent years, more Reform Jews are wearing it. In rare cases when Torah is read on Friday evening in some Reform congregations, worshipers are encouraged to put on the *tallit*. In recent years, a small number of women in the Reform,

Reconstructionist, and Convervative movements have begun to wear the *tallit*, although it is more common for girls to wear them for the *bat mitzvah* when she is called to the Torah. While there is some difference of opinion among Orthodox authorities as to whether women are permitted to wear the *tallit*, it seems clear that they are indeed permitted to do so unless they are doing so to show an extra measure of piety.

The *tallit* must be made of the same cloth as the *tzitzit*. However, woolen *tzitzit* may be used, regardless of the type of cloth use for the *tallit*. The *tallit* should be put on with both hands. Before doing so, one should recite the blessing: "Praised are You, Adonai our God, Sovereign of the Universe who has made us holy with *mitzvot* and instructed us to wrap ourselves in *tzitzit*." Then the *tallit* is raised over the head, wrapped around one's shoulders (depending on the style of the *tallit*). It is also customary to wrap the *tallit* momentarily around one's head immediately following the recitation of the blessing. Some worshipers wear the *tallit* over their head for the entire service or for the recitation of the *amidah* ("the standing prayer," core prayer in Jewish liturgy) in order to increase their concentration. Afterwards the worshiper recites a set of prescribed verses.

REFERENCES

Donin, Hayyim Halevy. *To Be a Jew: A Guide to Contemporary Observance*. New York: Basic Books, 1991.

Klein, Isaac. *A Guide to Jewish Religious Practice*. New York: The Jewish Theological Seminary of America, 1979.

TASHLIKH. During the afternoon of the first day of Rosh Hashanah (or the second day if the first day falls on the Sabbath), it is customary, primarily among Ashkenazi Jews (originally of German origin), to go to any body of water, such as a river or lake, and recite psalms (118:5–9; 33; and 130) and the last verses of the prophet Micah (7:18–20) including: "You shall cast all their sins into the depths of the sea (Micah 7:19). Added to the recitation of these verses is the prayer, "May You cast all the sins of your people Israel into a place where they will not be remembered, nor counted, nor ever again minded." The ritual derives its name, *tashlikh*, from these verses, and some prayer books have constructed a prayer using words from this verse.

Individuals symbolically "cast out" their sins by emptying the pockets (which have been filled with bread crumbs) and turning out the cuffs of their clothing. Women shake their garments as well. While there are many interpretations for this custom, the basic symbolism is obvious. Just as the crumbs are taken away by the current of the water, the individual prays that his or her sins be carried out of God's sight so that they should not unduly influence God's decision to inscribe the individual in the book of life. It is the custom of some communities to do *tashlikh* only in bodies of water that have fish as the precarious nature of their environment reminds us of the fragile nature of our own.

Although there are various biblical and post-biblical references to prayers near bodies of water, the *tashlikh* ceremony probably did not exist prior to the fourth century. The ceremony is not mentioned in the Talmud, nor in the responsa of the *geonim* (community authorities who led the rabbinical academies in Babylonia from the sixth to the eleventh centuries). It first appears in *Sefer Maharil* of Rabbi Jacob Moëllin, known as the Maharil, who lived from 1355 to 1427. He claims that the ritual is connected to a midrash that suggests that as Abraham went with Isaac to Moriah, Satan tried to thwart them by placing a deep body of water in front of them. Undismayed, Abraham crosses over the water and continues with his task. By performing *tashlikh* near a body of water, we are reminded of Abraham's test as well. Moëllin discouraged using bread (as food for fish) as is the common practice today. Others suggest that the ceremony is done by water with the fish as witness to human behavior because the eyes of the fish never close—just like the unblinking eyes of God. In prayers that have been added to the ceremony, reference is made to evil spirits created by the sins of the individual, which cling to one's garments and should be shaken off.

The ceremony may simply have emerged as an outdoor folk activity that followed a full day of sitting inside the synagogue in reflective prayer. It is especially helpful to parents whose children have been sitting inside the synagogue. *Tashlikh* gives them the opportunity to run around outside without disturbing others. It also could be a reference to be casting out of Hagar and Ishmael (the Torah reading for the first day of Rosh Hashanah). It is her act of being cast out (*tashlikh*) that brings them to life-giving waters, a theme that is revisited in the *haftaraot* (readings from the prophetic literature that complement the Torah reading; see **haftarah**) for Yom Kippur, which includes verses from Micah and the entire book of Jonah. In the latter, water transforms life and renews it.

Some authorities fought against the ceremony, arguing that it contained superstitions. Others felt that the gathering in community might lead to sins such as gossip and tale-bearing and liaisons between men and women.

The Hasidim who lived in the Galician village of Bolehov marched to the river in a procession for *tashlikh* carrying lighted candles. The sun's setting rays mingled with the light of the candles. Then they lit small bundles of straw with the candles and placed these floating bundles of fire on the water. While creating a lovely sight, the waters swept away their sins and the fires burned them.

The Jews of Kurdistan actually jumped into the water and swam in it in order to be fully cleansed of their sins. In certain communities in Israel where there are no natural bodies of water, individuals gather near cisterns or wells containing water. However, in Safed, residents go on the roofs of their homes so that they can see the Kinneret. In some Oriental communities, *tashlikh* is said around a basin of water into which live fish are placed. It is important to note that *tashlikh* contributed to another false accusation against the Jewish community: poisoning the rivers.

For many years, most Reform congregations eschewed this ritual. In recent years, more congregations have adopted it, however. As most Reform congregations observe only one day of Rosh Hashanah, the ritual usually takes place in the afternoon whether or not it is the Sabbath.

REFERENCES

Chill, Abraham. *The Minhagim: The Customs and Ceremonies of Judaism: Their Origin and Rationale.* New York: Sepher-Hermon Press, 1979.

Goodman, Philip. *The Rosh Hashanah Anthology.* Philadelphia: The Jewish Publication Society of America, 1970.

TEFILLIN. The directive for putting on *tefillin*, or phylacteries as they are called in English, comes from Deuteronomy 6:8, where readers are told to "bind them for a sign upon your hand and as frontlets between your eyes." The ancient rabbis interpreted this instruction to put *tefillin* on the arm in order to recollect God's outstretched arm that brought the Israelites out of Egypt and opposite the heart to remind the Jewish people to subject itself to God's will. The other *tefillin* box is placed on the head, opposite the brain, to remind the individual that one's mental faculties should be subjected to Divine service.

The *tefillin* consist of two black leather boxes. Each box contains four passages from the Torah that mention the obligation of *tefillin*. These are the first two sections of the *shema* (Deuteronomy 6:4–9, 11:13–21; Exodus 13:1–10, 11–16). The box that is designed for the head has four passages in four separate compartments. However, they are written on one parchment in one compartment in the hand piece.

Tefillin are put on before the morning prayers and are not worn for the afternoon or evening service. However, they are worn during the afternoon service on Tisha B'av. *Tefillin* are not worn on the Sabbath nor on the major festivals. Yet, communities differ on this practice during the intermediate days of Sukkot and Pesach (Passover). Sephardic Jews (whose origin can be traced to Spain) do not put on *tefillin* during the intermediate days, but some Ashkenazic Jews (whose origins can be traced to Germany) do. Hasidic Jews follow the practice of the Sephardim. Similarly, the general custom in Israel is not to put on *tefillin* during the intermediate days of the festivals.

While the worshiper is standing, *tefillin* should be put on immediately following the *tallit*. Because nothing should come between the *tefillin* and the body, shirt sleeves are rolled up and hats are removed, although the head should still be covered by a **kippah**. The worshiper takes the handpiece first and places it over the muscle of the left arm (the right arm for people who are left-handed), with the *ma'abarta* (protuding part of the base that has the leather strap, the *retsuah*, threaded through it) toward the shoulder. The protruding part of the base on the other side should face the hand. The knot should face the heart. Before tightening the strap, one should recite this blessing: "Praised are You, Adonai our God, Sovereign of the Universe who has made us holy with *mitzvot* and instructed us to tie the *tefillin*." Then the *retsuah* is tightened and wound seven times over the arm between the elbow and the wrist. Depending on the custom of the community, some wind clockwise while others wind counterclockwise.

The headpiece is then placed over the head so that the box (*bayit*) is over the hair, with the outer edge not extending where the hair begins to grow. The *kesher* (knot) should rest on the base of the skull above the nape of the neck. After placing it properly, one recites this blessing: "Praised are You, Adonai our God, Sovereign of the Universe who has made us holy with *mitzvot* and instructed us concerning the *mitzvah* of *tefillin*." This is followed by the recitation of this text: "Praised is God's name whose glorious sovereignty is forever and ever."

After this blessing is made, the individual takes the remaining strap on the arm and winds it around the middle finger, twice on the lower joint and once on the middle joint. What still remains of the strap is wound around the palm. While doing this or immediately thereafter, one should recite this text from Hosea 2:24: "I will betroth you to me forever; I will betroth you to me in righteousness and justice, in kindness and mercy; I will betroth you to me in faithfulness; and you shall know Adonai." When this is wound properly, the name of God as *Shaddai* (Almighty) may be seen spelled by the hand.

At the end of the worship service, one removes the *tefillin* in the reverse order. First, the *retsuah* around the hand and finger is unwound. The headpiece is removed next and put away. There are a variety of acceptable methods for storing the *tefillin*. Most people wind the strap around the protusion at the base of the box; the strap should never be wound around the box itself. Finally the remainder of the *retsuah* is unwound and the handpiece is removed and similarly put away. Most people keep their *tefillin* in a special bag designed for that purpose. When putting the *tefillin* away, one should place the headpiece on the right and the handpiece on the left to make it easier when they have to be removed the next day. The *tefillin* are removed on Rosh Chodesh (the day that commemorates the new moon) following the Torah service and before the *musaf amidah* (the "standing" prayer in the additional service). In those communities where *tefillin* are worn during the intermediate days of festivals, they are removed before Hallel.

It is customary to kiss *tefillin* when one removes them from the storage bag as well as before one puts them away for storage once again. In addition, one should kiss the *tefillin* while saying these phrases during the morning service: *ozer yisrael bigvurah* (Who helps Israel mightily), *oter yisrael b'tifarah* (Who adorns Israel with majesty), *yismechu hashamayim vetagel ha-aretz* (the heavens rejoice and the earth is glad), *poteach et yadekhah* (open Your hand), and (twice) *ukshartem leot* (bind them as a sign). One should not sleep or eat while wearing *tefillin*.

A small part of the Jewish community uses two pairs of *tefillin*, wearing one from the beginning of the service until after the *amidah* ("standing prayer" which forms the core of the worship service) and the second for the remainder of the service. The standard *tefillin* are called "Rashi *tefillin*," named for the rabbinic commentator who determined the order of the verses placed inside. According to Rabbenu Tam (12th century, France), for whom the other version of *tefillin* are named, the order of these verses is slightly altered with the *shema* verse itself coming last, rather than next to last.

It is the general practice for males to begin to put on *tefillin* at the age of 13. While there is no prohibition against women using *tefillin* and there is evidence that women have done so in Jewish history, it remains basically a male ritual. However, a growing number of women in the Conservative, Reconstructionist, and Reform movements are performing this ritual. As early Reformers generally rejected the ritual of *tefillin*, this ritual is not observed frequently in Reform temples; nevertheless, an increasing number of Reform Jews have added it to their personal practices.

REFERENCES

Neiman, Moshe Chanina. *Tefillin: An Illustrated Guide*, translated by Dovid Oratz. New York: Feldheim Publishers, 1995.
Sandberg, Martin. *Tefillin*. New York: United Synagogue for Conservative Judaism, 1992.
Shinom, Eiden D. *Halachos of Tefillin*. New York: Feldheim Publishers, 1984.

TEVILAH. Ritual immersion in a *Mikvah* (ritual bath) is called *tevilah*. Jewish law requires such immersion following the menstrual cycle for women, prior to marriage for women, and following the release of bodily fluids, such as a nocturnal emission, for men. It is also used for the purpose of conversion for both men and women. Some use it to prepare for the Sabbath and holidays. While some view the use of the *mikvah* as a way of moving from impure to pure ritual states, *tevilah* is really about spiritual preparation and transformation rather than the states of ritual purity and impurity.

The *mikvah* must be built according to a set of specifications, and it must be filled at least partially with flowing waters. *Mikvah* literally means "living waters"; thus, ponds, lakes, rivers, and seas are natural *mikvaot* (plural of *mikvah*). The Talmud claims that the source of all water is the river that emerged from Eden. By immersing in the waters, people are reborn in the pure, innocent state of Adam and Eve.

In the case of the menstruant, immersion should take place after the completion of seven clean days. *Tehinnot*, women's prayers that evolved primarily in Europe from the sixteenth to nineteenth centuries, have been written for the *mikvah*. Often these are used by women to help prepare themselves for immersion. Before the immersion, the woman washes completely so that no particle of dirt can act as a barrier between the water and her body. With arms and legs spread and with eyes gently closed, the individual completely immerses herself in the water, making sure that her hair is completely submerged as well. After the immersion, the woman recites the blessing "Praised are You, Adonai our God, Sovereign of the Universe, who has made us holy with *mitzvot* and instructed us concerning immersion." She then immerses herself a second time. In some communities, three immersions are common, corresponding to the number of times the word *mikvah* appears in the Torah. Even among Orthodox Jews, ritual immersion following menstruation as a requirement before conjugal relations can be resumed in marriage is practiced less frequently than many of the other rituals. Some Conservative and Reconstructionist Jews follow this practice; however, few Reform Jews do so.

For conversion, witnesses are required. As traditional Judaism requires male witnesses, these men stand outside of the bath and listen carefully for the woman to immerse herself and recite the required blessings. In the case of conversion, immersion is required by all movements. Due to the philosophy of personal autonomy as advocated by proponents of Reform Judaism, some Reform rabbis may not require immersion. However, the tendency to require immersion for conversion is on the increase.

According to the laws of *niddah*, or family purity, which are related to the menstrual cycle, a woman makes her first trip to the *mikvah* prior to marriage in order to establish a pattern that she will follow during her married life. Some men choose to go to the *mikvah* before marriage as well. These laws are observed by Orthodox Jews and some Conservative and Reconstructionist Jews, but few Reform Jews. Often brides and grooms add the *shehecheyanu* blessing (a prayer that offers thanks to God for bringing individuals to that day) to the immersion ritual.

A scribe must also immerse himself prior to the writing of God's name in the Torah. Some Jews also attend the *mikvah* prior to Yom Kippur. Some add a blessing for the restoration of the Temple to the blessings said at the time of immersion.

Among Sephardic Jews, a visit to the *mikvah* is often festive and party-like. Many contemporary Jews have extended this custom by bringing friends, food, and wine to the *mikvah*.

REFERENCES

Adelman, Penina. "Nisan: Time to Redig Miriam's Well." *Genesis 2* (March–April 1983), pp. 6–12.

Diament, Anita. *The New Jewish Wedding*. New York: Summit Books, 1985.

Goldstein, Elyse. *Re-Visions: Seeing Torah through a Feminist Lens*. Woodstock, VT: Jewish Lights Publishing, 1999.

Kaplan, Aryeh. *Waters of Eden: The Mystery of the Mikvah*. New York: National Conference of Synagogue Youth/Union of Orthodox Jewish Congregations, 1976.

Koltun, Elizabeth, ed. *The Jewish Woman*. New York: Schocken Books, 1976.

TWELVE MONTHS OF MOURNING. This is the fourth stage of mourning (which includes the previous three) following the death of a loved one. The first stage is between death and burial, followed by **shiva** and **sheloshim**. If a parent has died, the period of mourning extends beyond these initial periods. The mourner continues to recite the **mourner's kaddish** (the memorial prayer) every day, three times a day in the presence of a *minyan* (prayer quorum). (The Reform movement generally does not require the presence of a *minyan*, although members of the movement have begun to reinstate this requirement.) In the Orthodox community, only men recite *kaddish*. Often, if a woman's parent dies, and particularly when there are no male descendants of the deceased, then the bereaved's husband may take on the responsibility of saying *kaddish*. Or the bereaved woman may engage a *kaddish zahger* (*kaddish* sayer) to say *kaddish* for eleven months. Recently, more Orthodox women have taken on the responsibility of saying *kaddish* even though they may not be counted in a *minyan*.

Some authorities recommend that *kaddish* should be recited for eleven months; others suggest that mourners recite *kaddish* for the full twelve months. The origin of this discrepancy is unclear. While it makes sense that the mourner should stop saying *kaddish* for a month prior to the ***yahrzeit*** (anniversary of death), this is not usually the reason that is given.

REFERENCES

Diament, Anita. *Saying Kaddish: How to Comfort the Dying, Bury the Dead, and Mourn as a Jew.* New York: Schocken Books, 1998.

Dobrinsky, Henry. *A Treasury of Sephardic Laws and Customs: The Ritual Practices of Syrian, Moroccan, Judeo-Spanish and Spanish amd Portuguese Jews of North America.* Hoboken, NJ, and New York: KTAV and Yeshiva University Press, 1986.

Lamm, Maurice. *The Jewish Way in Death and Mourning.* Middle Village, NY: Jonathan David Publishers, 1969.

Wieseltier, Leon. *Kaddish.* Alfred A. Knopf: New York, 1998.

TZITZIT. *Tzitzit* refers to the specially-wrapped fringes on each corner of the **tallit** *katan*, small *tallit* (or *arba kanfot* as it is also called), or *tallit gadol*, which is worn as a prayer shawl for morning prayers. The smaller *tallit* is generally worn as an undergarment by traditional Jewish men and should be put on as the first garment upon arising in the morning. Although some choose to wear it over their clothing, many others wear it over their undergarments. In the ancient world, *tzitziot* (plural of *tzitzit*) were attached directly to one's garments, which were four-cornered in order to fulfill the obligation "And you shall look at it [the fringes] and remember God's commandments" (Numbers 15:39). Now the *tallit katan* fulfills this obligation. One says the following blessing upon putting it on: "Praised are You, Adonai our God, Sovereign of the Universe, who has made us holy with *mitzvot* and instructed us concerning the obligation of *tzitzit*."

The *tallit* must be made of the same cloth as the *tzitzit*. However, woolen *tzitzit* may be used, regardless of the type of cloth used for the *tallit*. The *tzitzit* is attached at follows: At each corner of the garment, there is a hole about an inch or two from the hem. Four threads, three of which are of equal length and the fourth longer, are entered through the hole and folded over in order to make eight threads. Seven of these should be of equal length and the eighth, which is designated at the *shammash* (literally "the servant," or service thread) and used as the primary thread to tie the *tzitzit*, is longer than the rest. A double knot is made with the two sets of four threads. After the double knot, the *shamash* is wound seven times around the other seven. Another double knot is made and the *shamash* is wound eight times around the seven threads. A double knot is made once again and the *shamash* is wound around another eleven times. This process is repeated with thirteen rings. Then a fifth and final double knot is made. Each *tzitzit* should be the length of about 18 fingerbreadths, and the part containing the knots should make up approximately one-third of the total length.

The *tzitziot* are gathered together in one hand just prior to reciting the *shema*, reflecting the text which suggests that the Jewish people will be gathered from the four corners of the earth. While continuing to hold the *tzitziot*, some people cover their eyes with them during the recitation of the *shema*. As the *shema* is traditionally said in a sitting postion, this works easily. It is more difficult for most Reform Jews, as they stand for the recitation of the *shema*.

The *tzitzit* are kissed at various times during the worship service, as a way of expressing love and devotion for God. The *tzitzit* are kissed at the end of the *baruch she-amar* ("Praised are You who speaks") prayer, during the third passage following the *shema*—whenever the word *tzitzit* is said—and at the conclusion of this passage on the word *emet* (truth). In addition, it is kissed at the end of the succeeding passages on the words that conclude each section: *kayamet* (exists) and *olamei olamim* (eternally). This practice was rejected by Reform Judaism, but many Reform Jews have restored the custom in their personal practice.

REFERENCES

Donin, Hayyim Halevy. *To Be a Jew: A Guide to Contemporary Observance.* New York: Basic Books, 1991.

Klein, Isaac. *A Guide to Jewish Religious Practice.* New York: The Jewish Theological Seminary of America, 1979.

U

UNVEILING. While it is customary to wait at least eleven months before setting and then unveiling a tombstone, there seems to be no legal precedent for doing so—although authorities do mention it in the eighteenth century. It is customary among traditional Jews to wait twelve months. This custom probably emerged from the length of time for saying *kaddish* during the first year of mourning (see **mourner's *kaddish***). Following a specific law, Jews in some communities put up the stone as soon as possible following ***shiva***. In Israel, it is customary to do so following the period of ***sheloshim***. The authorities appear to agree that the unveiling must take place no later than twelve months after burial as the deceased is on the mind of the mourner during that period.

Because burial places were scattered in ancient times, markers were used as a sign to *kohanim* (priestly descendants) to avoid the area as they were prohibited from coming into contact with the dead. Once burial sites became clustered in cemeteries, the purpose of the marker, or stone, changed.

REFERENCES

Diament, Anita. *Saying Kaddish: How to Comfort the Dying, Bury the Dead, and Mourn as a Jew.* New York: Schocken Books, 1998.

Dobrinsky, Henry. *A Treasury of Sephardic Laws and Customs: The Ritual Practices of Syrian, Moroccan, Judeo-Spanish and Spanish and Portuguese Jews of North America.* Hoboken, NJ, and New York: Ktav and Yeshiva University Press, 1986.

Klein, Isaac. *A Guide to Jewish Religious Practice.* New York: The Jewish Theological Seminary of America, 1979.
Lamm, Maurice. *The Jewish Way in Death and Mourning.* Middle Village, NY: Jonathan David Publishers, 1969.
Wieseltier, Leon. *Kaddish.* Alfred A. Knopf: New York, 1998.

USHPIZIN. Introduced by the mystic Rabbi Isaac Luria in the sixteenth century, this custom emerges out of the teachings of the *Zohar.* An invitation is extended to "holy guests" to enter the *sukkah.* The elaborate invitation concludes with the special mention of one of the guests, as a different one is invited on each of the seven festival days. Each guest—Abraham, Isaac, Jacob, Joseph, Moses, Aaron, and David—represents one of the *sefirot*, the mystical emanations of God. As all of the guests were wanderers, the theme of wandering, which is reflected in the temporary nature of the *sukkah*, is also reflected in the *ushpizin.* Recently, some people have added seven women of the Bible to the "guest list." This list generally comprises Sarah, Rachel, Rebecca, Leah, Miriam, Abigail, and Esther. Some prefer an alternative list of women, who they feel may more appropriately reflect the individual *sefirot*: Miriam, Leah, Hannah, Rebecca, Sarah, Tamar, and Rachel.

REFERENCES

Goodman, Philip. *The Sukkot and Simhat Torah Anthology.* Philadelphia: The Jewish Publication Society of America, 1973.
Isaacs, Ronald. *Every Person's Guide to Sukkot, Shemini Atzeret, and Sinchat Torah.* Northvale, NJ: Jason Aronson, 1999.
Strassfeld, Michael. *The Jewish Holidays: A Guide and Commentary.* New York: Harper & Row, 1985.

V

VIDUI. Literally "confession," *vidui* specifically refers to the obligation of the individual to recite the confessional prayer at the beginning of Yom Kippur. It is the second step in reaching a state of repentance. The *vidui* captures the posture of the entire Yom Kippur liturgy. Thus, the confessional prayer is also recited on the day of Yom Kippur following the *amidah* prayer, the core prayer in the worship service. Other prayers that reflect this posture are also recited throughout the day: *Atah yodeah* (You know), *Atah mavene* (You understand), and *al chet* (for the sin). These prayers are recited during the evening, morning, and afternoon services on Yom Kippur. In addition, the *vidui* is the formulaic deathbed confession of the individual.

REFERENCES

Donin, Hayyim Halevy. *To Be a Jew: A Guide to Contemporary Observance.* New York: Basic Books, 1991.

Elbogen, Ismar. *Jewish Liturgy: A Comprehensive History*, translated by Raymond P. Scheindlin. Philadelphia: Jewish Publication Society, 1993.

Goodman, Philip. *The Yom Kippur Anthology.* Philadelphia: The Jewish Publication Society, 1971.

Greenberg, Irving. *The Living Way: Living the Holidays.* Northvale, NJ: Jason Aronson, Inc., 1998.

Klein, Isaac. *A Guide to Jewish Religious Practice.* New York: The Jewish Theological Seminary of America, 1979.

W

WEDDING RING. There is no specific reference to a wedding ring in the Talmud. However, it appears to have an ancient tradition. Saadiah Gaon (882–942) suggests that it finds its origin in Nehemiah 7:46 where "children of the rings" refer to those who cohabited while only betrothed (with the ring) but not yet married. Most contemporary scholars disagree with this claim and offer a variety of explanations. "Rings" (*tabbaot*) may have been a family name. Perhaps the ring was a Palestinian custom that was later introduced into Babylonian practice. One scholar dates the entry of the ring into Palestine in the seventh century and notes its appearance in Babylonia two centuries later. Another scholar suggests that the strange practice of performing the betrothal over a glass of wine with a ring inside of it may have led to the eventual adoption of the ring. However, this practice does not appear in the major medieval law codes. Regardless of its origin, the ring became a substitute for the gold coin or other article of value that a man used to purchase his wife from her father. The ring need only be worth a *pe'rutah* (a low valued coin). It is a monetary equivalent that is one of the three legal acts of acquisition— and the only one that is exclusively practiced today. The other two forms are legal contract (not to be confused with **ketubah**) and sexual intercourse (not to be confused with **yichud**).

The placement of the ring (and its exchange) is an important part of the wedding ritual as it represents part of the legal requirements for ***kiddushin***. The ring must be of plain metal, without stones. This requirement prevented any doubt as to the value of the ring or the possibility of the bride accepting the marriage under false premises. However, it does not have to be of gold. This requirement is maintained by most Orthodox rabbis and a large number of Conservative rabbis. Few Reform rabbis makes this requirement. An engraved ring is often permitted by all. As the ring became a symbol, even traditional authorities loosened the requirements. This also opened up the possibility of new interpretations of legal requirements. Thus, the ring symbolized the anticipated harmony of the marriage, which should not be marred in any way. The plain band—free of stones or embellishment—helped to communicate the idea that all stand equal before God in marriage, whether rich or poor. Sometimes, a bride uses one ring for the ceremony and then wears a different ring following the ceremony.

In order for all to see, the groom places the wedding ring on the index finger of the bride's right hand. This also serves to communicate that this ring is more than just a gift. It is quite possible that this finger is used because rings were worn on that finger in prior generations, a practice that is experiencing a revival. Then the groom recites the traditional formula of consecration: "By this ring, you are consecrated to me, according to the law of Moses and Israel." While a ring may be placed over a glove, it is preferable for nothing to come between the ring and the person wearing it. As this part of the ceremony is crucial, because the giving and accepting of a ring in the presence of witnesses affirms the legal aspect of marriage, it is important that the groom use a ring that actually belongs to him. Although it is not recommended by the authorities, he may borrow a ring for the ceremony, provided that his bride knows that it is a borrowed item.

Specially designed oversized rings that resemble houses are often used during wedding ceremonies so that witnesses can actually see the placement of the ring on the bride's finger. This gave rise to the creation of wedding rings by artisans as ritual objects. It is now common for craftspeople to make rings that contain Hebrew names in raised letters or quotations from the Song of Songs. A double-ring ceremony is frequently performed at Conservative, Reform, Reconstructionist, and some Orthodox weddings. At such a ceremony, the bride and groom each exchange rings. Orthodox couples who choose to use two rings are often advised by the rabbi to have the bride give the groom the ring after the ceremony is concluded. In a double-ring ceremony, the bride places a ring on the ring finger of the groom's left hand (after she has received the groom's ring). Often she does not say anything. In some cases, brides recite a reworking of the phrase said by the groom or recite a line from the Song of Songs, such as "I am to my beloved as my beloved is to me."

During the Talmudic period (and presumably before that era), the marriage ceremony was divided into two parts. The first is called *kiddushin* (separation, consecration) or *erusin* (betrothal). The groom effected the betrothal by handing over something of value to the bride in the presence of witnesses reciting the formula "Behold you are consecrated to me with this ring according to the law of Moses and Israel." After the rabbis combined the two aspects of the ritual, they moved the giving of the ring into the *kiddushin*, the wedding ceremony itself.

REFERENCES

Biale, David. *Eros and the Jews: From Biblical Israel to Contemporary America.* Los Angeles: University of California Press, 1997.

Lamm, Maurice. *The Jewish Way of Love and Marriage.* San Francisco: Harper and Row, 1980.

Routtenberg, Lilly S., and Ruth R. Seldin. *The Jewish Wedding Book.* New York: Schocken Books, 1967.

Y

YAHRZEIT. From the Yiddish meaning "year-time" (called *anos* or *nahalah* among many Sephardim, descendants of Jews from Spain), the *yahrzeit* marks the Hebrew date of the anniversary of a death. It is not counted from the time of the interment. However, there was some debate as to whether this method for dating holds true for the first *yahrzeit*, especially in cases where the burial took place three years after the death. Some people use the secular calender to reckon the date of *yahrzeit*. The first Scriptural reference to *yahrzeit* appears in Judges 11:40: "It was a custom in Israel that the daughters of Israel went yearly to lament the daughter of Jephthah, the Gileadite, four days a year." However, the origin of this ritual is somewhat unclear. Its name would indicate that it is of German origin and it is first evidenced in writings of the sixteenth century. It may have evolved from similar rites among German Catholics or as an extension of the commemoration of the anniversary of deaths of great individuals in Jewish history, such as Moses, Gedalia, or some of the great rabbis. (Gedaliah was governor of Judah, appointed by the Babylonians after the fall of Jerusalem in 586. He was murdered shortly after his appointment, a day now marked as a fast day on Tishrei 3.) The practice of marking the death of individuals came later to the Sephardim than the Ashkenazim, those Jews who hail from Central and Eastern Europe.

While *yahrzeit* is observed for one's parent, some authorities extend this practice to include the other five close relatives for whom mourning is enjoined: brother and sister, son and daughter, and spouse. Although the *yahrzeit* date is to be fixed by the calendar, in those cases where one is unsure about the precise date of death, one may choose an appropriate date to observe the *yahrzeit* and then continue to do so from year to year.

On the day marking an individual's *yahrzeit*, the mourner recites the **mourner's *kaddish*** at every service during the day as the chief expression of that commemoration, beginning with the evening service of the night before and concluding with the afternoon service of the day itself. In traditional contexts, the mourner may be invited to lead the worship service. In addition, the mourner lights a twenty-four-hour memorial candle, which symbolizes the verse "the soul of a human is the lamp of God." The lighting of the candle probably dates to the medieval period. There is no specific ritual required for the lighting of the memorial candle. Alternatively, an electric light may be used. If the *yahrzeit* occurs on a day when Torah is read, the mourner is often honored with a Torah ***aliyah*** or asked to read the ***haftarah***. In some congregations, the mourner is called to the Torah on the Sabbath prior to the *yahrzeit*. At that time, the memorial prayer *El maleh rachamim* is also chanted. While fasting is not a commonly observed practice, some fast on the day of *yahrzeit*. Some large synagogues have adopted the practice of saying the memorial prayer after the Torah reading at the afternoon service on Shabbat for those who will observe a *yahrzeit* during the ensuing week.

The *Shulchan Arukh* suggests that it is a *mitzvah* to fast on the *yahrzeit* of one's parent (Orach Chaim 568:7). It is also a *mitzvah* to fast on the *yahrzeit* of a prominent teacher (Mishnah Berurah 568: 46). However, the fast is prohibited when it conflicts with select days of celebration, such as Shabbat or Rosh Chodesh, or days of preparation, such as Fridays before Shabbat or the day prior to Yom Kippur or Tisha B'av. Fasting is directly connected to the concept of *teshuvah* (repentance). One fasts in order to ask for pardon of the dead.

The *yahrzeit* is marked by the anniversary of the Hebrew date of death, rather than on the secular calendar. However, some do follow the secular date. If one is uncertain of the date, one may choose a date and mark that date as the anniversary in years following. Among many Reform congregations, *yahrzeit* is only observed on the Shabbat closest to the actual date of the *yahrzeit*.

REFERENCES

Donin, Hayyim Halevy. *To Be a Jew: A Guide to Contemporary Observance.* New York: Basic Books, 1991.
Klein, Isaac. *A Guide to Jewish Religious Practice.* New York: The Jewish Theological Seminary of America, 1979.
Rabinowicz, Tzvi. *A Guide to Life.* Northvale, NJ: Jason Aronson, Inc., 1989.

YICHUD. Best described as "togetherness in privacy," *yichud* is the ritual that concludes the wedding nuptials. According to traditional Jewish law, a man and a woman who are not married to one another may not be alone in a room together. Thus, following the conclusion of the wedding ceremony, bride and groom retire to a room together where they symbolically consummate their marriage. They act as husband and wife for the first time. There they also break the traditional wedding fast. Although no specific foods are required, in Ashkenazic communities (referring to those Jews whose ancestors are from Central and Eastern Europe), the couple often the breaks the fast with chicken soup, while Sephardim (those Jews whose ancestry is from Spain) often eat doves as a symbol of marital peace. While at one time, *yichud* included sexual intercourse, this aspect of private communion has not been in practice for many centuries. *Yichud* must be "witnessed" by two individuals who testify that the couple has been alone for the first time. The ritual allows both individuals to mark their transition in personal status. In most Reform, Conservative, and Reconstructionist congregations, this practice is seldom acknowledged.

REFERENCES

Diament, Anita. *The New Jewish Wedding.* New York: Summit Books, 1985.
Goodman, Philip and Hanna. *The Jewish Marriage Anthology.* Philadelphia: The Jewish Publication Society of America, 1965.
Gross, D. C., and E. R. Gross. *Under the Wedding Canopy: Love and Marriage in Judaism.* New York: Hippocrene, 1996.
Lamm, Maurice. *The Jewish Way in Love and Marriage.* San Francisco: Harper and Row, 1980.
Routtenberg, Lilly S., and Ruth R. Seldin. *The Jewish Wedding Book.* New York: Schocken Books, 1967.
Westheimer, Ruth, and Jonathan Mark. *Heavenly Sex: Sexuality in the Jewish Tradition.* New York: Continuum Publishing Group, 1996.

YIZKOR. Literally "He shall remember," referring to God, *yizhor* is the opening word of the memorial prayer said for one's closest relatives who have died. It is the custom in many synagogue communities, perhaps a superstitious holdover from the Middle Ages in Europe, for individuals with living parents to leave the place of worship during the section of the service that contains *yizkor* prayers and is therefore called the *yizkor* service. *Yizkor* is usually read after the Torah reading; however, some congregations have moved it to the afternoon. Many Sephardim do not say *yizkor* at all. Some scholars suggest that the practice evolved for other reasons: to avoid arousing the jealousy of those whose parents are dead; to prevent those who do not have to say *yizkor* from saying it in error; and to avoid placing individuals in the awkward position of remaining silent while those around them are worshiping. Others suggest that we find it as early as the second book of Maccabees (12:43–45), which mentions that Judah collected funds that he sent to Jerusalem as a sin offering for those who had died "in that he was mindful of the resurrection. For if he had not hoped that they were slain should have risen again, it had been superfluous and vain to pray for the dead. Likewise, he perceived that there was great favor laid up for those that died godly, it was a divine and holy thought. Whereupon he made a reconciliation for the dead, that they might be delivered from sin."

The *yizkor* service continues to have wide appeal as it "helps to bind the generations together in filial piety" (Klein, 140). The *yizkor* service takes place on the last Day of Passover and Shavuot as well as on Shemini Atzeret and the Day of Atonement. As a result of differences in calendation, the Reform movement generally offers the *yizkor* prayer one day earlier than the rest of the Jewish community outside Israel, except on the Day of Atonement, which is observed on the same day throughout the Jewish community. However, in the order of prayers known as the *Machzor Vitry* (1208), the Yom Kippur memorial prayers are mentioned without any reference to the other holidays. Later, the custom developed to recite these prayers on days in which the Torah portion dealing with the obligation of supporting the poor is read (e.g., the last days of Passover and Shavuot and the eighth day of Sukkot).

REFERENCES

Chill, Abraham. *The Minhagim: The Customs and Ceremonies of Judaism, Their Origins and Rationale.* New York: Sepher-Hermon Press, 1975.

Goodman, Philip. *The Yom Kippur Anthology*. Philadelphia: The Jewish Publication Society of America, 1971.
Klein, Isaac. *A Guide to Jewish Religious Practice*. New York: The Jewish Theological Seminary of America, 1979.

Index

Boldface page numbers indicate location of main entries.

Adot hamizrach, 84
Adret, Solomon ben Abraham, 72
Afikomen, 108–9
Afterlife, 19
Aggadah, 81
Agunah, 86
Akedah, 21
Aliyah, **1–4**; Bar Mitzvah, 8–9; *benchen gomel* and, 13; blessings of the dawn, 20; children, 88–89; naming ceremony for girls, 28; tallit wearing, 128; Torah reading and, 36, 75; wedding rituals, 5; at *yahrzeit*, 148
Alkabetz, Rabbi Solomon Halevi, 69–70
Amidah, 15, 17, 48, 64, 100, 129
Ana Adonai, 94
Ana Bakoach, 70
Aravot, 93–94
Arba kanfot, 88, 137
Arks, xv
Asher yatzar, 19
Ashkenazic community: blessings, 14, 16, 21, 49, 65; death rituals, 147; dietary laws, 12; Friday night table rituals, 54; Kabbalat Shabbat, 69; *kiddush*, 80; prayers, 128; as source of rituals, xxi; *tashlikh*, 129; *tefillin*, 132; Torah reading, 57; wedding rituals, 4, 85, 149
Atzei chayim, 3
Atzilut, 111
Aufruf, **4–6**

Baal keriah, 74
Babylonian Jews, 76, 87, 143
Baraita, 81
Bar/Bat Mitzvah, **7–10**, 38–40, 53, 129
Barekh, 109
Barukh shepatarani, 8–9
Bayit, 132
Bedecken, **10–11**, 85
Bedikat chametz, **11–13**
Benchen gomel, **13**
Benchen licht, 59

Ben Ish Chai, 8
Beriah, 111
Berit olam, 116
Betar, 16
Bet din, 7, 43–44, 46, 78
Beth El, 40
Betulta, 87
Bimah, 1, 3–4, 31, 36
Birkat chattanim, 119
Birkat hachodesh, **14–15**
Birkat hagomel, 13
Birkat hamazon, **15–17**, 55, 103, 115, 119
Birkat kohanim, **17–18**, 23
Birkat levanah, 82
Birkot hashachar, **18–22**
Birth of children, xviii, 27, 106, 116–17
Bitul chametz, 12, **22–23**
Biur chametz, 12, **23**, 98
Blada, 116
Blessing of children, 17, **23–24**, 54, 89, 120
Blessings: *benchen gomel*, 13; benediction, 17–18, 23; *birkat hachodesh*, 14–15; of bread (*See* Bread, blessing of); of candles, 59–61; of children, 17, 23–24, 54, 89, 120; of the dawn, 18–22; *duchanen*, 48–49; of fruit, 111; of girls, 27; grace after meals, 15–17, 55, 109; of the home, 35; immersion, 43; of *matzah*, 109; of the moon, 82–83; of the sun, 81–82; *tefillin*, 132–33; *tevilah*, 135; before the Torah reading, 75; wedding, 23, 27, 86, 115–16, 119–20, 135; of wine, 17, 55, 64–65, 80–81, 108–9
Blowing the shofar, **24**, 92
Boys: Bar Mitzvah, 7–10, 38; birth of, 116–17; circumcision, xii, 27–30, 42–43, 53, 105; Confirmation, 38–40; Consecration, 41–42; firstborn, 105–6; haircutting, 33. *See also* Children
Bread, blessing of: grace after meals, 15–17; Passover, 12, 22–23; prior to eating, 63–64, 103; Shabbat, xvi, 55
Breaking of the glass, ix, **24–27**, 86
Brit banot, **27–28**
Brit bat, 27
Brit edut, 27
Brit kedusha, 27
Brit milah, xii, 27, **28–30**, 42–43, 53, 105
Brit rekhitzah, 27
Brit Sarah, 27
Building a *sukkah*, **30–32**, 140
Burial, 92–93, 99–100, 118, 121, 125, 139. *See also* Death rituals

Calendar, Jewish, 14, 81, 150
Candle lighting, xiii, xviii, 54, 59–61, 148
Chabad Hasidim, 8
Chagigah, 108
Chair of Elijah, 29
Chalakah, **33**
Chalitzah, **33–35**
Challah, xvi, 55, 64, 114. *See also* Bread, blessing of
Chametz, 11–13, 22–23, 97–98
Chanukat habayit, **35**
Chanukiyah, 60
Charoset, 109
Chatan bereishit, **35–36**, 36, 88
Chatan Torah, 36, **36–37**, 88
Chazan, 48–49
Chemdat Yamim, 110
Chevra kaddisha, 118, 122, 125–27
Chiddur mitzvah, xiv
Children: birth of, xviii, 27, 106, 116–17; blessing of, 17, 23–24,

INDEX

54, 89, 120; Confirmation, 38–40;
Consecration, 41–42; education
of, xvii, 41–42; at funerals, 92; *kol
hane'arim*, 88–89; *mamzerut*
status, 46; redemption of firstborn, 105–6; at *seder*, 108–9; *tashlikh*, 130. *See also* Bar/Bat
Mitzvah; Boys; Girls
Chuppah, 26, 36, **37–38**, 84, 86, 119
Circumcision, xii, 27, 28–30, 42–43,
53, 105
Cleansing covenants, 27
Community, ritual and, xx–xxi
Confession, 141
Confirmation, 9, **38–40**, 41
Consecration, 39, **41–42**
Conservative congregations: *aliyah*,
4; Bar/Bat Mitzvah, 9–10; blessings, 21; Confirmation, 40;
Consecration, 39; conversion, 43;
death rituals, 91–92; divorce, 46;
head coverings, 88; *kiddush*, 60;
naming ceremonies, 27; *omer* period, 114; *sukkah*, 31; Torah
reading rituals, 63; use of rituals
in, xi; wedding rituals, 5, 78, 86–
87, 144; women, xii, 4
Conversion, **42–44**, 135
Counting ritual, 113
Custom, xvi

Day of Atonement. *See* Yom Kippur
Death rituals: afterlife, 19; *aliyah*, 4;
blessings, 23; for death of parent,
99–100, 136, 147; eulogies, 66,
91, 122; fasting, 148; Kabbalat
Shabbat and, 70; *kaddish*, 92–93,
99–101; *levayah*, 91–93; mirrors
and, 122; preparation of the
body, 125–27; remarriage of
widow, 33–35; *sheloshim*, 117–18;
shemirah, 118–19; *shiva*, 73, 115,
117, 121–23; tearing of garments,
72–73; twelve months of mourning, 136–37; unveiling of the
tombstone, 139; *yahrzeit*, 4, 15,
33, 100, 136, 147–49; *yizkor*, 150
Devar Torah, **45–46**, 115
Dietary laws, xii, 12
Divorce, **46–48**, 78–79
Dosick, Rabbi Wayne, xx
Duchanen, 18, **48–49**
Dwelling in a *sukkah*, 30–32, 140

Eastern European Jews, xx
Edot haMizrach, xxi
Education, xvii, 8, 41–42
Egers, Samuel, 39
Eisenstein, Judah, 128
Elijah's cup, **51–52**, 109
Elohai neshamah, 19
Emet Ve-emunah, xi
Erev Shavuot, 39
Erusin, 83–84, 145
Ethiopian Jews, 112
Etrog, 93–95

Fasting at *yahrzeit*, 148
Fast of the firstborn, **53–54**
Finkelstein, Louis, 16
Folk religion, ritual from, x–xi, xiii
French Jews, 40
Friday night table rituals, 23, **54–55**
Funerals, 91–93, 100. *See also* Death rituals

Gabbai, 2, 74
Gadlu Adonai, 74
Gaon, 14, 16, 21
Gedaliah, 147
Gelilah, **57**, 62, 75
Gematria, 5, 111

Geonic period, 14, 16, 21, 72, 130
Gerut, 42–44, 135
Get, 46–47
Girls: Bat Mitzvah, 7–9, 38–39; blessing, 89; Confirmation, 38–40; naming ceremonies, 27–28; redemption of firstborn, 106; *tallit* wearing, 129. *See also* Children
Grace after meals, 15–17, 55, 109

Hadasim, 93–94
Hadlakat hanerot, xiii, xviii, 54, **59–61**
Haftarah, **61**; *aliyah* and, 2, 5; Bar/Bat Mitzvah, 10; *birkat hachodesh*, 15; on Shabbat, 75; *tashlikh*, 130
Hagbah, 57, **62**, 75
Haggadah, 107, 109
Hakafot, xv, **63**, 74
Hallel, 109
Ha-mappil prayer, 77
Hamol, 127
Hamotzi, 55, **63–64**, 81, 103, 126
Hanasi, Rabbi Judah, 65
Hanukkah, 59, 60–61
Harachaman, 16
Harvest ceremonies, 112–14
Hasidic community, 8, 15, 115, 131–32
Hatafat dam brit, 29, 43
Hats, removal of, xi, xx. *See also* Kippah
Havdalah, xiii–xiv, 24, 59, **64–66**, 80
Heraclitus, xviii
Hesped, **66–67**
Hillel sandwich, 109
Hodu, 94
Hol hamoed, 73
Holocaust, xi
Horowitz, Isaiah, 72
Hoshanah Rabbah, 71
Hoshanot, 95

Introspection and ritual, xi–xii
Ishmael, Rabbi, 22
Israel Independence Day, 111, 113
Israeli traditions, 10, 29, 48–49, 109, 131, 139
Isserles, Moses, 72

Jerusalem, ix, 24. *See also* Temple, destruction of
Jew-by-Choice, 42–44
Jewish renewal movement, xxi
Judah, Rabbi, 21

Kabbalat Shabbat, 54, **69–71**, 121
Kaddish, 92–93, 99–101, 117, 128, 136
Kaddish zahger, 136
Kallah, 36
Kaplan, Mordecai M., x, xii, 9
Kapparah, **71–72**
Karaites, 14
Karpas, 108
Keriah, **72–73**, 92, 122
Keriat haTorah, **73–77**
Keriat shema al hametah, **77–78**
Kesher, 132
Ketubah, 11, 46, **78–79**, 85–87
Kiddush, **79–81**; Friday night table rituals, 55; over wine, 65; at *seder*, 108; in *sheva berakhot*, 119; in the synagogue, xiii, 60; wedding ceremonies, 5; women, xviii
Kiddush hachamah, **81–82**
Kiddush levanah, xix, **82–83**
Kiddushin, **83–87**, 143–44
Kimcha de-Pisha, 97
Kinyan, 85
Kippah, xi–xii, xx–xxi, **87–88**, 132
Kittel, 85
Kohanim, 2, 48, 105–6, 139
Kol chamira, 12, 22
Kol hane' arim, 42, **88–89**
Kol Nidre, 128

Korekh, 109
Kosher dietary laws, xii
Krauskopf, Joseph, 39
Kurdistan, 29, 131

Lag B'Omer, 33, 85, 113
Lauterbach, Jacob, 37
Lekha Dodi, 54, 69–70
Lel ikd ill Yas, 29
Lentils, 116
Levayah, **91–93**. *See also* Death rituals
Levirate marriage, 34
Lillith, 30
Lithuanian Jews, 10
Lubavitch Hasidim, 15
Lulav, **93–95**
Luria, Rabbi Isaac, 72, 140

Ma'abarta, 132
Maariv, 77
Machir, Moses ibn, 128
Machzor Vitry, 5, 150
Maftir, 2, 5, 10, 35, 61
Maggid, 109
Maharil (Rabbi Jacob Mollin), 130
Maimonides, Moses, 20, 39, 75
El malei rachamim, 15, 92–93
Mamzerut, 46
Maot chittin, **97**
Maror, 109
Marriage. *See* Wedding ceremonies
Matzah, **97–98**, 109
Matzah mitzvah, 98
Mechilah, 92
Mekhirat chametz, 12, 23, **98–99**
Men: candle lighting, 59; death rituals, 118, 125, 136; divorce, 46–47; *kiddush levanah*, 83; recent movement for, xix; *sukkot*, 31; *tzitzit*, 128; wedding rituals, 78
Meturgeman, 75
Mezuzah, 35

Midrash, 30, 130
Mikvah, 43, 126–27, 134–36
Mincha service, 18, 48
Minhag hamakom, 3
Minyan, xiv, 1, 13, 48, 119, 136
Miriam's cup, 110
Mirrors, 122
Miscarriage, xviii
Mi sheberekh, 9
Mit'assekim, 126
Mitzvah, 7, 21, 48, 53, 125, 148
Mohel, 28–30
Moroccan Jews, 8, 10
Motzi matzah, 109
Mourner's *kaddish*, **99–101**, 117, 136, 139, 148. *See also* Death rituals; *Kaddish*
Musaf Amidah, 24
Musaf services, 14, 18, 48–49, 95

Nahalah, 147
Naming ceremonies, 27–28
Netilat yadayim, 19, 55, **103–4**, 126
New Moon rituals (Rosh Chodesh), xviii, 14, 70, 133
Niddah, 135
Niggun, 36
Nirtzah, 110
Nissuin, 37, 84. *See also Chuppah*
North American Jews, xx

Omer offerings, 112–14
Oriental Jews, 116, 131
Orlah, 33
Orthodox congregations: Bar/Bat Mitzvah, 9; death rituals, 73, 136; *devar Torah*, 45; divorce, 46; haircutting, 33; *kapparah*, 71–72; *minyan*, 1; naming ceremonies, 27–28; *tallit* wearing, 129; *tevilah*, 135; wedding ceremonies, 85, 144

Palestinian traditions, 76, 143
Palm branches, 93–95

Passover rituals: *aliyah*, 3; *bedikat chametz*, 11–13; *biur chametz*, 23; *chametz*, 12, 23, 98–99; Elijah's cup, 51–52, 109; evening prayer, 77; fast of the firstborn, 53–54; *matzah*, 97–98; *seder*, 51, 53, 97–98, 107–12; *tefillin*, 132; wheat money, 97
Persian Jews, 29
Pesach. *See* Passover rituals
Pesukei D'zimra, 18
Petuchowski, Jakob J., xx
Philo of Alexandria, 29, 31
Phylacteries *(tefillin)*, xi, xvii, 8, 41, 127–28, 131–34
Pidyon haben, **105–6**, 116
Pirke Avot, 114–15
Piyyut, 8, 36, 70
Prayers: *aliyah* and, 4; Bar/Bat Mitzvah, 9; in community, xiv; confessional, 141; *Hamol*, 127; *kabbalat Shabbat*, 54; *kaddish*, 92–93, 99–101; *keriat haTorah*, 74; women's, 135; at *yahrzeit*, 148; *yizkor*, 150
Prayer shawl *(tallit)*, xii, 38, 41, 89, 127–29, 137
Pri Etz Hadar, 110

Rachtzah, 109
Rape, xviii
Reconstructionist movement: *aliyah*, 2–4; Bar/Bat Mitzvah, 9; birth of children, 106; blessings, 21; conversion, 43; death rituals, 92, 121; naming ceremonies, 27; *sukkah*, 31; updating rituals in, xx; wedding rituals, 5, 86, 144
Reform movement: *aliyah*, 2–4; Bar/Bat Mitzvah, 9, 38; birth of children, 106; blessings, 18, 21–22; blowing the shofar, 24; candle lighting, 59–60; *chametz* rituals, 12; circumcision, xii, 28–29; Confirmation, 38–40; Consecration, 42; conversion, 42–44, 135; death rituals, 91, 93, 100, 121, 136, 148; divorce, 46; Eastern European Jews, xx; Friday night table rituals, 54; *havdalah*, 65; head coverings, 88; individual choice in, xiv; Kabbalat Shabbat, 70; *minyan*, 1, 13; naming ceremonies, 27; *omer* period, 113; palm branches, 95; *sedarim*, 110; sermons, 45; skullcaps in, xi–xii; *sukkah*, 31; *tallit*, 128, 138; *tashlikh*, 131; *tefillin*, 134; Torah reading, 61, 74, 76; updating rituals in, xi, xiii–xiv, xix, 1; wedding rituals, 5, 26, 78, 85–86, 144
Renewal congregations, 71
Retsuah, 132–33
Ritual: changes in, x–xi, xiii, xviii–xxii; community and, xii–xiv, xx–xxi; definitions of, xiv–xvi; from folk religion, x–xi, xiii; function of, xvii–xviii; how-to aspect of, xix–xx; meaning of, xv; place in Judaism, ix–x, xx; for self-reflection, xi–xii; teaching of, xvii
Rosh Chodesh, xviii, 14, 70, 133
Rosh Hashanah, 24, 71, 129

Sacrifices, 22, 71
Salonika, 30
Sanhedrin, 14, 79
Seder, 51, 53, 97–98, **107–12**
Seder Hayom, 128
Seder peridah, 46
Sefer keritut, 46
Sefirat haomer, 70, 110, **112–14**
Sefirot, 140
Self-reflection and ritual, xi–xii
Sephardic traditions: Bar/Bat Mitzvah, 9; births, 27; blessings, 13–

INDEX

14, 16, 21; circumcision, 30; death rituals, 92, 117, 122, 147, 150; *omer* period, 113; prayers, 15; prayer shawl, 128; ritual in, xxi; *seder*, 107, 109; *tefillin*, 132; Torah reading, 57, 62, 75; wedding rituals, 5, 26, 86, 149
Seudah shelishit, **114–15**
Seudat mitzvah, 10, 26, 53
Seven Days of Feasting, 17, **115–16**, 119. See also *Sheva berakhot*
S'gan, 74
Shabbat: *aliyot*, 3; Friday night table rituals, 23, 54–55; Kabbalat Shabbat, 54, 69–71, 121; *kiddush*, 80; lighting of candles, xiii, xviii, 54, 59–61, 65; prohibitions, 24; *seudah shelishit*, 114–15
Shabbat Mevarkhim, 14
Shaliach tzeebor, 15
Shalom Aleikhem, 54
Shalom nekavah, 27
Shalom zakhar, **116–17**
Shamash, 60, 137
Shasha, 116
Shavuot, 39, 112
Shehechayanu prayer, 80, 135
Sheloshim, 73, **117–18**, 122
Shema: *birkot hashachar*, 22; at circumcision, 30; conversion, 43; head covering, 87; on retiring for the night, 77, 116; Shabbat, 74; *tzitzit* and, 138
Shemini Atzeret, 42
Shemirah, **118–19**
Shemurah matzah, 98
Sheva berakhot, 17, 27, 86, 115–16, **119–20**
Shevu'a haben, 30, 116
Shimon bar Yochai, Rabbi, 33
Shiva, 4, 73, 115, 117, **121–23**
Shluggen kapparos, 71–72
Shulchan Arukh, 72

Shulkhan orekh, 109
Siddur, 15, 42
Signs vs. symbols, xiv–xv
Simchat bat, 27
Simchat Torah, 42, 62–63, 76, 88–89
Six Day War, ix, xxi, 88
Siyyum, 53
Skullcap *(kippah)*, xi–xii, xx–xxi, 87–88, 132
Slaughter of fowl, 71
Sofer, 46–47
Sukkah, 30–32, 140
Sukkot, 3, 42, 71, 93–95, 132
Symbols, xiv–xv

Taanit bekhorim, 53–54
Tachanun, 66, 91, 93
Tahara, **125–27**
Taharat hamishpacha, xvii
Tallit, **127–29**; in *aliyah*, 3; children and, 89; daily wear, 137; use by boys, 41; use by women, xii; in wedding ceremonies, 38, 85. See also *Tzitzit*
Tallit gadol, 137
Tallit katan, xx, 88, 127–28, 137
Talmudic period, 73, 84
Targum, 75
Tashlikh, **129–31**
Tefillin, xi, xvii, 8, 41, 127–28, **131–34**
Tefillin derasha, 9
Tehinnot, 135
Temple, destruction of, ix, xiii, 24–26, 72, 95, 112–13
Temple cult, 18
Temple period, 112
Teshuvah, 148
Tetragrammaton, 18, 48
Tevilah, **134–36**
Tipat dam, 29, 43
Tish, 45

Tisha B'av, xi, 83, 128, 132
Torah: children and, 88–89; circuit of, xv; dressing of, 57; explanation of, 45–46; palm branches, 95; processional, 63; raising of, 57, 62, 75; reading of, 1–5, 35–37, 40, 61, 73–77, 128; study of, 19–20, 30. *See also Aliyah*
Tu Bishevat *seder*, 110–11
Twelve months of mourning, **136–37**
Tzafun, 109
Tzidduk hadin, 92–93
Tzitzit, 3, 62–63, 75, 127–28, **137–38**. *See also Tallit*

Unveiling, **139–40**
Urchatz, 108
Ushpizin, **140**

Veula, 30
Vidui, **141**

Washing of hands, 19, 55, 103–4, 108–9, 121–22, 126–27
Water, 43, 126–27, 129–31, 134–36. *See also* Washing of hands
Wedding ceremonies: *aliyah*, 4; *aufruf*, 4–5; *bedecken*, 10–11; blessings, 23, 27, 86, 115–16, 119–20, 135; breaking of the glass, ix, 24–27; of childless widows, 33–35; *chuppah*, 37–38; grace after meals, 17; honeymoons, 116; *ketubah*, 11, 46, 78–79; *kiddushin*, 83–87; rings, 84, 86, 143–45; seven days of feasting, 115–16; *yichud*, 149
Wedding ring, 84, 86, **143–45**
Wine, blessing of, 17, 55, 64–65, 80–81, 108–9
Wohl, Rabbi Samuel, 41
Women: *aliyah*, 2, 4; blessings and, 21, 80; candle lighting, xviii, 54, 59; Conservative congregations, xii, xiv; conversion, 42–43; death rituals, 118, 125, 136; *devar Torah*, 45; divorce, 46–47; hats, 87; *minyan*, xiv, 1; new rituals for, xviii; *omer* season, 113; ritual baths, 134–36; Rosh Chodesh, xviii, 14, 83; *sedarim*, 110; *sukkot*, 31; *tallit* wearing, 128–29; *tashlikh*, 130; *tefillin*, 134; Torah reading rituals, 63; *ushpizin*, 140; wedding rituals, 26, 78, 86–87, 144–45

Yachatz, 108–9
Yahrzeit, 4, 15, 33, 100, 136, **147–49**
Yarmulkeh, 87. *See also Kippah*
Yehi ratzon, 21
Yemenite Jews, 30, 70, 109
Yeshu'a haben, 30, 116
Yetzer harah, 12
Yetzirah, 111
Yevamah, 33–34
Yichud, 84, 86, **149**
Yizkor, **150–51**
Yom Ha-atzmaut (Israel Independence Day), 111, 113
Yom Hashoah (Holocaust Memorial Day), xi, 113
Yom Kippur (Day of Atonement): *aliyot*, 3; blessing of children, 23; blowing the shofar, 24; building a *sukkah*, 31; *kiddush levanah* and, 82–83; prayers, 141; slaughtering a fowl, 71; *tallit* wearing, 128; *yizkor* service, 150

Zakkai, Rabbi Yochanan ben, 24
Zemirot, 55, 114
Zeroa, 108
Zeved habat, 27
Zimmun, 16–17
Zohar, 33, 113, 117, 122

About the Author

KERRY M. OLITZKY is the Executive Director of the Jewish Outreach Institute in New York City. He is the author of numerous books and journal articles, and has written extensively in the field of American Jewish History. His previous publications include *Reform Judaism in America: A Biographical Dictionary and Sourcebook* (Greenwood, 1993), which he coauthored with Lance J. Sussman and Malcolm H. Stern and *The American Synagogue: A Historical Dictionary and Sourcebook* (Greenwood, 1996).